GW00384521

Christianity

Religion

for the Layman

To Jenny

With very warm wishes

Peter

By Peter Stevens

Christianity and Religion for the Layman

Contents

Chapter 1: Introduction: The Four Aims.

This little book has four general aims. The first is to show the thinking agnostic that there is a God and there is a life after this one. I have met many good people in this life whose attitude lies along the lines of "No evidence - no belief"! But at least one hopes that they are open to reason. My aim will be to provide some overwhelming evidence for the existence of God, although there is never going to be absolute proof. My second aim is to demonstrate to regular church goers who have a belief in God, that scientific progress means that the world may not always be exactly as the Bible describes. I intend to show that I have a firm belief in God, in Jesus Christ and, in particular, the Resurrection, but that there are some aspects of Christianity that are, in my opinion, not quite in line with some of the Anglican Church's teaching. There are some people who take every word of the Bible literally. This group tends to be intolerant and blinkered, unwilling even to listen to other points of view. They also tend to be dismissive about the discoveries of science especially over the subjects of creation and evolution. When pressed, some of them tend to become ever more dogmatic and entrenched in their positions. At its worst this can overflow into what I would call "Spiritual Abuse" where a vulnerable or young person is told what would be best for him or her and that they would go to Hell if they do not believe in Jesus. This can be very damaging for someone with, say, mental health problems. At the other end of the scale is a group whom we might call militant atheists, who wish to have nothing to do with any religion. I intend to show that the correct way forward is somewhere in between these two extreme positions.

When we talk about the past, we shall need a global calendar or a way of providing meaningful dates. Jesus Christ was supposed to have been born in the Year One, and all dates refer to years before or after this huge event. In fact as we shall see in Chapter 5, Jesus was probably born some 4 or 5 years earlier but that is by the way for the moment. It used to be that events before the birth of Christ were referred to as BC or "Before Christ". Events after the birth of Christ were AD or *Anno Domini* or "The Year of our Lord". BC and AD have now been replaced by BCE and CE, where CE refers to "Christian Era" or "Common Era". You can conveniently take your pick on that one depending upon whether you count yourself as a Christian or not. Thus BCE refers to "Before the Christian Era" or "Before the Common Era". In this book I shall use BCE and CE.

My own background is that of a scientist. I was born in the Channel Island of Jersey in May 1940 just before the German Occupation of the island. My parents and I, as a new born baby, escaped from the island just before the Occupation. We returned in 1945 after World War II and in Chapter 3, I shall describe something ominous that we found in our home at that time. A degree in Natural Sciences, Physics, at Magdalen College, Oxford completed my education. My abiding interest continues to be astronomy and cosmology, together with mathematics. My working life was spent in the classroom teaching mathematics mainly at secondary schools. I did not study theology, but have read many books on the subject in subsequent years, and now have an abiding interest in that as well. My intention is to keep the discussion on as simple lines as possible. But it is as a scientist, that I have always been interested in religious questions such as: "What happens if anything after death?", "How does it all come about?", "What is behind it all?", "Is there anyone out there?", "Why are we here?", or simply just, "Why?" In the same way, a pure scientist might simply ask "How?" Further questions could be: "Can science and religion go hand in hand or must they be always in conflict with each other?" and "Can religions other than Christianity lead to God?" Thus I have been drawn to religion in the hope that it might provide at least some of the answers.

Stephen Hawking was my exact contemporary at Oxford, studying for the same degree course. We must have been to the same lectures, but to my great regret I never actually met him. He continued to work throughout his life and at the time of his death in early 2018, he was working on a book that was published after his death: "*Brief Answers to the Big Questions*". The first three chapters of this book are entitled "Is there a God?", "How did it all begin?" and "Is there other intelligent life in the universe?" These are just some of the questions that I shall endeavour to think about in this book.

But along an often difficult path, I have found that religion does attempt to provide answers but they are ones that can seem, at times, to be at variance with science. And yet I am sure that there are answers!　I was brought up as an Anglican, and it is an Anglican that I have remained.　This is partly because I feel more at home with the Church of England, but also because there is a greater sense of freedom with one's beliefs.　A good religious discussion, with full respect for differing views is something that I find can be hugely worthwhile and enjoyable.

In this book my third aim will be to show that religion and science need not be that far apart, and that it is possible to bring the two sides closer together.　Until the time of the Reformation in the 16th century, there was relative peace between various religious groups and science.　The Roman Catholic Church taught that the Earth was the centre of the universe.　The Sun, the Moon, the five known planets, Mercury, Venus, Mars, Jupiter and Saturn all revolved around the Earth, and everyone was happy with that.　Then with the advancement of science, it all started to become uncertain.　One of the first battles was between Galileo and the Roman Catholic Church in the early 17th century.　He had invented a primitive telescope in 1610 and it soon became clear to him that the Earth was not the centre of the universe, but rather it revolved around the Sun as did all the other planets.　Only the Moon revolved around the Earth.　This put him on a collision course with the all-powerful Roman Catholic Church and he decided to retract in order to keep his job and position.　To-day, it is proven that the Earth is a rather small planet, revolving around an average star, the Sun, on the outskirts of the Milky Way, one of many galaxies throughout the Universe.

In the middle of the 19th century there was great debate about the origin of the Earth.　According to Genesis, the first book in the Bible, the Earth was created by God not long before Adam and Eve. An enterprising Bishop, by the name of Ussher, then proceeded to work out when this might be and came up with the year 4004 BCE. Indeed, many Victorian Bibles have this date printed on the first page of Genesis. It is not a particularly difficult exercise to make a few basic assumptions, and then add up all the ages of Abraham's ancestors, even allowing for their preposterous longevity (Methuselah supposedly achieving 969 years of age!) going back to Adam as given in Genesis, to arrive at about 4000 years BCE. Yet we know from Jericho, and other ancient cities of civilizations going back to at least 7000 BCE, that human history goes back many thousands of years before that. We now know that the Earth itself is far, far older - the latest estimate puts the Earth at some 4.56 billion years old. Much of this can be ascertained by the scientific process of carbon dating. This is just one example of how science and religion seemed to draw further and further apart. In more recent years, they have been starting to come together again, but there is still a long way to go. In the past, the Church has made the error of preaching many certainties which science then proceeds to show are groundless. I shall have more to say about this in later chapters. The "Theory of Everything" or T.O.E. in science suggests the idea that it is possible to explain everything. We are a lot further along the path of explaining the world than we were in, say, Newton's time. But there remains a long way to go, so we should continue to persevere. My belief is that there really is a T.O.E. although there are certain ideas such as the "Big Bang" which is supposed to explain how the Universe came into being, that are, at least for the present, beyond the understanding of the human mind. In addition, God must surely be included in T.O.E. Also, we now know a lot more about the various subatomic particles, such as the quark, than we did when I was a student in the early 1960s. But will we ever find the ultimate particle? I rather doubt it. The science of cosmology, which the study of the Universe including how it all began, is fascinating, but is beyond the scope of this book. I shall skirt round the subject in Chapter 4 when we shall consider whether there is a God and if so, whether it is necessary to have God in order to have the Universe that we live in. For those who might be interested, I urge them to read Stephen Hawking's *The Universe in a Nutshell*, David Filkin's *Stephen Hawking's Universe* or Gillian Straine's *Science and Religion.*

In the chapters to come, we will examine the various interactions between science and religion. There will be frequent quotations from the New International Version of the Bible, and I shall explain the significance of this version in Chapter 2. There have been many books on this topic that have tried to sort out some of the problems. *In my experience, a lot of these books ask many of the right questions clearly and then fail to give any sort of meaningful answer. Either the questions are not answered at all, or else the answer is so twisted and convoluted that the average reader is left more confused than ever.* In my view, all sincere questions should be given reasonable consideration, and if the person being questioned does not know the answer, or, indeed, if no-one knows the answer, this should be frankly and humbly admitted.

At this stage, I am giving the first of many quotations from the Bible and it comes from the first Epistle of Peter:

Always be prepared to give an answer to everyone who asks you to give the reason for the hope that you have. But do this with gentleness and respect, keeping a clear conscience, so that those who speak maliciously against your good behaviour in Christ may be ashamed of their slander. (I Peter 3: 15 – 16).

Conversely, during church sermons, many controversial questions are avoided, for fear of turning people away. In this book many of the same questions will be asked, and then I shall endeavour to give clear meaningful answers as far as I am reasonably able to do so. In particular, in Chapter 7, I shall tackle the all-important topic of the Resurrection, upon which the whole of the Christian faith depends. I make no claim to universal knowledge, and there will be times when the reader will wish to differ from the commentary given here. In this I would go further: there will be some readers who will firmly disagree with some of my conclusions. I have no problem with this because that is what makes life so much more interesting. It also has to be admitted that there will remain some questions for which there is, as yet, no real answer at all. All one can hope to do is to encourage people to think and to question. It may well be the case that we take three steps forwards and then two steps backwards, but at least there will be progress. We may also find, as many scholars have found, that the more we study ancient documents, the more questions we are likely to have.

But the way forward, surely, is to listen to other opinions that may be markedly different from one's own, have a good think about it and then gradually to move forward. My fourth aim is to encourage people to do just that. If good worthwhile discussions turn out to be the case, as a result, in however small a way, then this book will have succeeded.

Chapter 2:
The Bible.

The Bible consists of 66 books, 39 books in the Old Testament (O.T.) and 27 in the New Testament (N.T.). In fact many of the books in the N.T. are quite short making it only a little over a quarter of the length of the O.T. Since the time of about the third century CE when the N.T. was being put together, the Bible has been a tremendous source of teaching and inspiration to mankind. Both the O.T and the N.T. contain a wonderful collection of stories of human suffering, endeavour, sacrifice, hope and the sheer joy of life. Whether these stories are true or are mythical, they nevertheless form a vital part of our culture and are to be treasured. There are times, especially in the O.T., when it becomes very difficult if not impossible to separate fact from exaggeration and pure mythology. So many of the phrases or sayings in the English language originate from the Bible. Thus in my opinion, all children should be encouraged to have some knowledge of the Bible whether they are from a Christian background or not. Nevertheless, we have to face the fact that, whether we like it or not, there are some stories of the Bible that are simply *not literally nor historically true*. Also, as we shall see, there are some teachings in the O.T. that simply cannot and should not be taken at face value. These teachings may have been relevant to the people living in Biblical times, but they would be seen to be "politically incorrect" to-day, when we face different challenges. Anyone who thinks otherwise is going to have great difficulty with some of my arguments in this book. At all events, the Bible should not be taken literally as a manual for day to day living. The Bible should be seen as a wonderful library of books with a huge variety of material.

Throughout this book, I will take numerous quotations from the Bible. Each quotation will be taken from the New International Version, which is an updated Bible, because it is easier for the reader to understand the underlying meaning. I was actually brought up on the old King James version, (that is King James I), which is a translation in the language of the time. Nevertheless, there are times when I still love the language and poetry of the King James version. An example comes from St John's Gospel in Chapter 14:

"Verily, verily, I say unto you....." (John 14: 12), (King James Bible)

"I tell you the truth......" (John 14: 12), (New International Version).

One day we may have a version that begins the verse as *"Look here, chaps...."*, or *"Look here, guys...."*.

The O.T. consists of a huge array of Psalms, teachings and stories, and it is simply not possible to determine to what extent and how many of the stories are historically accurate. This collection of 39 books can broadly be divided into four main parts:

1. The first five books of the Bible, that is, Genesis, Exodus, Leviticus, Numbers and Deuteronomy, are called the "Torah" and contain many important stories about the origins of the

people of Israel. The Torah is particularly important and central to the Jewish Faith. This early part of the Bible covers the Creation and then the stories of Noah, Abraham, Isaac, Jacob, Joseph and Moses. It also contains the 10 Commandments and many aspects of the Law as applied to those early days. Deuteronomy ends with the death of Moses.

2. The next 12 books follow the history of Israel from about 1,200 BCE until about 400 BCE. These are Joshua, Judges, Ruth, I and II Samuel, I and II Kings, I and II Chronicles, Ezra, Nehemiah and Esther. This section begins with Joshua, the successor to Moses, who led the Children of Israel across the River Jordan and then it describes the conquest of Canaan. There then follow numerous stories of the history of Israel with all their ups and downs. The last book, Esther, is curious because it is one of only two books in the Bible not to mention God! In fact Nehemiah came after Esther in time and the book describes how Nehemiah helped to organise the rebuilding of the walls around Jerusalem after the return from exile. This goes up to around 433 B.C.E. and is historically the end of the O.T.

3. The next 5 books can best be described as the Poetry and Wisdom books in the Bible. They are Job, Psalms, Proverbs, Ecclesiastes and the Song of Songs. The book of Psalms is the longest book in the Bible and consists of a mass of sacred songs, poems and prayers. The book of Proverbs is just that – a series of concise often witty pieces of common sense and wise sayings that we can use to-day. The Song of Songs is a poem about sexual love and is the other book in the Bible not to mention God.

4.   Finally, the remaining 17 books of the Old Testament are all supposedly written by "The Prophets". The four "major" prophets are Isaiah, Jeremiah, Ezekiel and Daniel. Interposed between Jeremiah and Ezekiel is The Lamentations of (supposedly) Jeremiah, which is another short book of poetry. Then the remaining 12 books, Hosea, Joel, Amos, Obadiah, Jonah, Micah, Nahum, Habakkuk, Zephaniah, Haggai, Zechariah and Malachi are known as the "minor" prophets. Most of these are quite short books with a lot of poetry in them, and some of these prophets are fairly unknown and obscure.

These Hebrew Scriptures, as they are known, are likely to have come into existence gradually, and then the stories were handed down over many generations. The process of editing probably took place over the period from about the 5th to the 2nd centuries BCE, and in their final form, the books became known as the "Canon" or the official agreed list.   All the 27 books in the N.T., which we will come to later, were written by about 125 C.E.   Then by about 250 C.E. all the books of the Bible were compiled into the Canon and were generally recognised as being inspired.   Finally the books in the O.T and the N.T were divided up into the chapters that we now have by Stephen Langton, (c. 1150 – 1228), Archbishop of Canterbury. There are a total of 929 chapters in the O.T. and 260 chapters in the N.T. The Bible was further divided up into verses around the middle of the 16th century by Robert Estienne, a French printer, and there are a total of 31,173 verses in the whole Bible. Whether the stories in the O.T. were historically true or not is not that important. They stand in their own right.   A classic example is the well-known story of Noah and The Flood as told in Genesis, the first book of the Bible.   There are a number of stories from folk memory of great floods. They would have caused huge disruption amongst communities and would have been well remembered. Curiously, in this case, we have a good idea of what may well have happened. Geologists tell us that the Black Sea was a large inland lake until about 7,500 years ago, when suddenly it changed to being salt water. It seems that there was a huge in rush of water over what is now the Bosphorus. This may have been the result of a large earthquake, or, more likely, the ending of the last ice age when sea levels rose alarmingly, filling the inland lake and making it very much larger, resulting in what we now call the Black Sea. If we use carbon-dated mollusc shells from the submerged shoreline at a depth of about 500 feet on the edge of the Black Sea, we find that they divide into two groups. There are the older freshwater shells that are 7,800 or more years old and saltwater shells that are 7,300 or less years old. This indicates that the freshwater lake was inundated by salt water around 7,500 years ago, or about 5,500 BCE. It seems that a natural dam at to-day's Bosphorus may have suddenly given way. It has been estimated that some ten cubic miles of seawater a day roared into the Black Sea, then some 500 feet lower. The sea would have pushed inland by about a mile a day forcing the inhabitants to flee. Thus there came about what the inhabitants would have described as a large catastrophic flood. Hence we have the origin of a story whereby an enterprising man, call him Noah, did have or did build an "Ark" on which he set forth over the flood waters with his wife and family and perhaps a small selection of animals. Finally, the flood subsided to some extent, and the Ark came to rest on the mountains of Ararat according to Genesis 8: 4. Mount Ararat, 16,854 feet above sea level, happens to be the highest mountain in Turkey. It is a dormant volcano in the area being some 200 miles south east of the Black Sea. In fact there are smaller mountains in between the Black Sea and Mount Ararat, so if there is any historical basis to this story, the Ark may have come to rest somewhere nearer the Black Sea but still within the general area of the mountains of Ararat. Thus it would be reasonable to look for any possible remains of the Ark much nearer to the Black Sea rather than on Mount Ararat, as many have tried to do. There are plenty of loose ends, but in essence, the story of Noah could well have had some historical background. The biblical story would have been much exaggerated in its telling over the generations, but we can see how it may well have come about. Also, at 5,500 BCE, this is not so long ago that it would be forgotten, but long enough for the story to be passed down over a number of generations and thus become exaggerated.

There are numerous other gripping stories in the O.T., for example: Abraham about to sacrifice his son Isaac, the boy David fighting the giant Goliath, Daniel in the den of lions, and Jonah being swallowed by a whale and surviving. They are part of our culture and we must hope they stay that way. We have no real way of deciding whether these stories were historically true or not. My belief is that some were pure legend while others may have been founded on fact but got rather over-blown in the telling over many years. However, the story of Jonah and the whale must be legend and is best looked upon as a colourful parable. I shall not make a great deal of further reference to the O.T. – it is the N.T. that, I believe, is far more important for Christians in the search for the ultimate truth about God. The idea of everlasting love from God does not come out in much of the O.T. It is not until Isaiah Chapter 54 that God's feeling of a great love for humanity starts to come through. By contrast, the N.T. shows Jesus as a supreme symbol of a Divine Love.

Before we move on to the N.T., we need to be aware that some Bibles contain a third section known as the "Apocrypha", which is usually sandwiched in between the O.T. and the N.T. Apocrypha literally means "hidden". The Apocrypha consists of some 14 books and they generally refer to the period between the O.T and the N.T. from about 400 BCE till about 70 CE. The exact number of books given in the Apocrypha of different Bibles can vary a little depending upon the selection chosen by different branches of Christianity. These books were not in the original Hebrew Bible, and the reader will not find them in most Bibles to-day. Although not without interest, Christians do not accept that these books have divine authority. There is no reference to any of them in the N.T.

The New Testament begins with the story of Jesus and his followers from about the year 6 BCE until his death in about 30 or 33 CE. The first books in the N.T. are the four Gospels, Matthew, Mark, Luke and John, all really important books, and I shall return to these later in this chapter. The fifth book is the book of the Acts of the Apostles. This is an historic account of the adventures and teachings of the apostles after the death of Jesus, up until the time when St Paul reached Rome about the year 62 CE. This book is almost certainly written by the same author who wrote the Luke Gospel and can be thought of as Luke Volume II. The reasons for this are their similar style and in particular, the fact that both books are written to one "most excellent Theophilus". The Book of Acts begins:

In my former book, Theophilus, I wrote about all that Jesus began to do and teach. (Acts 1:1)

There then follow all the Epistles or letters to various churches or groups of Christians in different places explaining more about Jesus, and giving many practical hints about how to live a good life. The first 13 have Paul's name attached to them; that is Romans, I and II Corinthians, Galatians, Ephesians, Philippians, Colossians, I and II Thessalonians, I and II Timothy, Titus and Philemon, although it is now thought probable that he was not the author of some of the later Epistles. We can be reasonably sure that Paul was the author of I Thessalonians, his probable first letter written about 50 CE. This was followed by Galatians, II Thessalonians, I Corinthians, Romans and II Corinthians with Philippians as his last letter, written from prison about 62 CE. The brief and personal letter to Philemon was also probably written by Paul. The consensus of biblical scholars holds that the letters to the Ephesians, Colossians, I and II Timothy and Titus are possibly post-Pauline letters written by a follower in his name, very likely based on notes or fragments of letters left by Paul. It was known that a number of early Christians tried to forge letters using Paul's name. In fact there is a warning from Paul about possible forgeries of his name:

Concerning the coming of our Lord Jesus Christ and our being gathered to him, we ask you, brothers, not to become easily unsettled or alarmed by some prophecy report or letter supposed to have come from us, saying that the day of the Lord has already come. (II Thessalonians 2: 1 – 2).

I and II Timothy and Titus are known as the Pastoral Letters, because they are rather more personal and are directed to leaders of the Church rather than a general congregation. Most scholars think that these were not written by Paul because the style is different although the content is consistent with Paul's theology. Quite likely they were written by disciples of Paul, some years after his death but based on excerpts of letters written by Paul.

The next book is the Epistle to the Hebrews, whose author is unknown.   There then follow a further seven short Epistles reputedly by James, Peter (2 Epistles) John (3 Epistles) and Jude. The James Epistle may have been written by the James who was Jesus' brother, and who appears in the Acts of the Apostles and some of Paul's Epistles; and the very short Epistle of Jude may have been written by another of Jesus' brothers. If nothing else, Jude claims to be the brother of James in the very first verse of his Epistle. Whether the Epistles of Peter and John were written by the disciples of that name is not known, but scholars think it unlikely. Finally, we come to the last book in the Bible, The Revelation of St John the Divine. This is a very difficult book for the layman to understand, being all about visions and symbols and focussing on the end of the world when Christians believe that God will reign supreme.

It is the four Gospels that I wish to concentrate on. A part of one of the Gospels is nearly always read in church services. Each Gospel presents Jesus in a slightly different way and thus we can view Jesus from four different angles.

1. **Mark's Gospel** is the shortest, being just 661 verses. It was probably the first Gospel to be written in about 65 – 70 CE,

although in the Bible, it is the second book of the N.T coming after Matthew's Gospel. Unlike the other Gospels, there is not a lot of teaching in Mark and it concentrates more on what Jesus *did* rather than what he said. Furthermore, Jesus often appears to be in a great hurry in Mark: often we have "And immediately.... or "straight away..." as if he is the all action man. The Gospel may have been written by John Mark who appears briefly in the Acts of the Apostles (see Acts 13: 13) and who was the companion of the leading disciple Peter towards the end of Peter's life. Tradition states that Peter was crucified in Rome sometime in the early 60s CE. Tradition also holds that John Mark wrote the Gospel in Rome, writing down the story as he had heard it directly from Peter. See also I Peter 5:13 when Peter refers to "my 'son' Mark." They were not related but this was a way of stating that they had a strong friendship. Mark's Gospel has some rough edges to it, but, being the first to be written, it is generally thought to be the most authentic, and is thus an invaluable document. It seems likely that the last page or so of Mark's Gospel has gone missing. The Gospels ends abruptly at Chapter 16 Verse 8. I shall return to this matter in Chapter 8 when we examine the Resurrection.   7

2. **Matthew's Gospel** is the first book of the N.T and it shows Jesus very much from a Jewish angle. There are many references to the O.T. and the Gospel sometimes goes out of its way to show how a prophecy in the O.T. has come to fruition. An early example in the Gospel refers to the Virgin Birth. This was foreshadowed by Isaiah:

Therefore the Lord himself will give you a sign: The virgin will be with child and will give birth to a son, and will call him Immanuel. (Isaiah 7: 14).

There will be more on the Virgin Birth in Chapter 5. There is a lot of teaching in this Gospel including the Sermon on the Mount. It also denounces the Pharisees very forcefully for their hypocrisy. Although the Gospel is ascribed to the disciple Matthew, the author is unknown, and is almost certainly not the disciple Matthew. It contains 1068 verses and was probably written about 80 – 90 CE. This Gospel emphasises that Jesus is the Messiah, the Son of God, and that Jesus both fulfils and transforms the law God gave to Israel through Moses. The author of this Gospel used Mark as one of his primary sources, so that 90% of Mark is reproduced in Matthew. However, much of the detail has been edited and sometimes shortened, so that some of the background, as given in Mark, is missing. This Gospel was a favourite of the early church, but, curiously, it tends not to be the favourite to-day. This is possibly because much of the teaching in it can be quite heavy going.

3. **Luke's Gospel** is the longest, 1149 verses, and is in many ways the most complete. It is the only Gospel to have a sequel, this being the Acts of the Apostles, as stated above. The first two chapters contain several stories that are unique being related to Jesus' birth and early life. Luke often cross-references events to dates in outside Roman history. He appears to be a cultivated Gentile who converted to Christianity. There is a full account of Jesus' adult life from his baptism onwards including many miracles and parables. Luke is the Gospel that has the most number of parables

including some of the longest parables, such as the Prodigal Son and the Good Samaritan. It is aimed more for the Gentiles, and like Matthew, was probably written about 80 – 90 CE. The author, Luke, was probably Paul's companion for parts of Paul's later travels, including his final journey to Rome. Evidence for this comes in the so-called "we" sections of the Acts: 16:10 – 17, 20:5 – 15, 21:1 – 18, and 27:1 – 28:16. These sections imply (but do not prove) that Luke was with Paul for these parts of his journeys. He has been known as the Beloved Physician and may well have been Paul's general companion and doctor:

"Our dear friend Luke, the doctor, and Demas send greetings." (Colossians 4: 14).

This shows that Paul may well have depended on Luke to keep him company. There is some doubt that Paul was the author of Colossians, but this verse does sound authentic. Also, given that Luke was a doctor, it may also explain why he was interested in a good number of healing miracles in his Gospel. Luke's Gospel shows that Jesus was the Saviour of all, and it gives the clearest picture of Jesus as a human being. There are more stories about women in this Gospel, for example, the stories about Martha and Mary. He is also particularly concerned with minority groups, the poor, children and the oppressed.

The above three gospels are known as the Synoptic Gospels because of their similarity and the fact that they used many of the same sources. "Synoptic" comes from a Greek word meaning "seen together".

4. **John's Gospel** is quite different and contains many stories that do not appear in the Synoptics.   It has generally become known as the "Fourth Gospel".   Only about 8% of John's Gospel is repeated in the Synoptics.   Some well-known examples of stories that are unique to John include: The first miracle of changing water into wine, the one-to-one meeting with Nicodemus at night, the conversation with the Samaritan woman, which we will come on to in Chapter 6 and the raising of Lazarus, also in Chapter 6 of this book.   There are only two parables, the Good Shepherd, (John 10: 1 – 18) and the True Vine (John 15: 1 – 8).   There are, however, several rather long and complex sermons.   It emphasises that Jesus was sent into the world by God to be its Saviour.   It was written later than the other Gospels probably right at the end of the first century CE. The Gospel contains 878 verses and may have been written by the disciple John, or perhaps someone who knew him well. Tradition states that that John lived to extreme old age spending much of his life in Ephesus, while he wrote or dictated the Gospel, but there is no solid evidence for this.   Alternatively, John's Gospel may have been written by someone quite different, but we can be reasonably sure that it was written after the other Gospels.   It is also possible that John's Gospel may have had more than one author, just one of which was the disciple John himself.   The others may have been disciples of John.   Parts of the Gospel show a remarkable familiarity with the countryside of Palestine, this being evidence that this was John himself writing and being an eyewitness.   In addition, the later contributors may have done quite a lot of editing.   There appear to be two endings to the Gospel: John 20:   30 – 31 and John 21:   24 – 25.   Thus it appears that John 21 was written by a different author sometime later and is probably an appendix.

The Gospel is the most theological and, it has to be admitted, anti-Jew. For example, in John 8: verse 44, Jesus declares that the Jews are the children of the Devil.

I stated earlier that Matthew draws heavily on Marks's Gospel. Luke does the same, but to a lesser extent, and in both cases, they edit what Mark has written. Thus, for any story that is in all three Synoptic Gospels, I generally find it best to go to the Mark version in the first instance, where the story is at its most basic and unedited. Matthew and Luke also have some 270 + verses that are thought to have come from a common source that was unknown to Mark. Scholars refer to this as "Q" standing for "*Quelle*" which is a German word for source, this being mainly about the sayings of Jesus, and it has now been lost. Unfortunately, "Q" has nothing to say about the Passion and Resurrection of Jesus, where both Matthew and Luke follow Mark. Finally, both Matthew and Luke have a good number of verses that are unique to their respective Gospels, some 330 or so verses that are found only in Matthew and another 500 or so verses that are found only in Luke. In this we must include the Infancy stories. These are the first two chapters of Matthew and the first two chapters of Luke, which are unique and quite different from each another, as we shall see in Chapter 5. There are only about 50 or so verses that are unique to Mark, that were not used by either Matthew or Luke. As stated above, John's Gospel comes from quite separate sources and has a number of stories that do not appear in any of the other Gospels. To sum up for Matthew and Luke, we can say:

Matthew = Mark + Q + M

Luke   = Mark + Q +   L

where M and L refer to material that is unique to Matthew and Luke respectively.   All this implies that Mark came first and that Matthew and Luke drew heavily on Mark.   However, the order in the Bible gives the Gospel Matthew coming first. There was a strong early tradition that Matthew wrote the first Gospel in Hebrew or Aramaic and this makes good sense if he was writing primarily for Jewish readers. Nevertheless, the balance of probability still favours Mark being the first gospel to be written. The hypothetical source "Q" was probably quite early perhaps about 50 – 60 CE.   We can make out a time line for the life of Jesus and the various books of the New Testament along these lines.

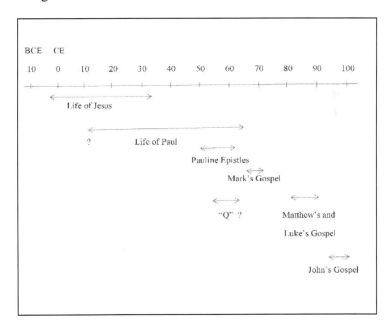

Matthew, Mark, Luke and John together are known as the Canonical Gospels; that is, the Gospels that were accepted to be part of our Bible to-day. During the first four centuries C.E. there were a number of "Gospels" and other books that were making the rounds purporting to be about Jesus and the apostles. Various councils took place towards the end of the fourth century, such as that of Laodicea (369 CE), Hippo Regius (393 CE) and Carthage (397 CE), during which it was decided which books should be included in the "Canon". Thus our modern Bible came into being. In the first centuries of Christianity, there were numerous other texts, which although they professed apostolic authority, were nevertheless clearly apocryphal or mythical.

But there was one text that may have been a "near miss". This is the so-called "Gospel" of Thomas. It contains 114 sayings of Jesus which were reputed to have been written down by the disciple Thomas. Scholars now think that it was written towards the end of the second century A.D., and so the author could not have been the disciple Thomas. The document was unknown, except by name, until December 1945, when a jar containing 13 leather-bound manuscripts was discovered by accident and dug out of the ground, near Nag Hammadi in Egypt. The jar had been buried sometime about the fourth century CE. Amongst other ancient writings of early Christians, the jar contained the "Gospel" of Thomas and at the time this was sensational. Even the opening words are intriguing:

"These are the secret sayings which the living Jesus spoke, and which Didymus Judas Thomas wrote down."

Many of the sayings can be found in the Canonical Gospels perhaps in a slightly different form; others are new but entirely plausible. There are also similarities with the hypothetical source "Q", mentioned above. Similar to "Q", this "Gospel" has nothing to say about the Passion or Resurrection of Jesus. However, over a third of the sayings 114 sayings of the "Gospel" of Thomas probably came directly from "Q".

Other non-Canonical "Gospels" include the Infancy "Gospel" of James which I shall refer to again in Chapter 5. This "Gospel" was written towards the end of the second century and has nothing to do with the disciple James, nor the James who is referred to as Jesus' brother. There is also the Infancy "Gospel" of Thomas which is nothing to do with the "Gospel" of Thomas mentioned above. There are a number of other non-Canonical "Gospels" including the "Gospel" of Peter, the "Gospel" of Philip, the "Gospel" of Mary Magdalene and several more. These were written in the second century CE or later still. Apart from material taken from the four Canonical Gospels, the other stories contained appear to be obvious forgeries, and are examples of folk religion of the time. While these stories are of interest as early Christian literature, they are mostly implausible and therefore very largely can be disregarded.

The question now arises as to how far we can take the material in the New Testament as historically accurate. My working hypothesis is that if something is in the text that is incidental to the story, it will almost certainly be historically correct. Furthermore, if the text does not coincide with the interests and agenda of the early Christian community, or even is at odds with those interests, then that text is also very likely to be authentic. A classic example of this is the following two verses:

A certain young man, wearing nothing but a linen garment, was following Jesus. When they seized him, he fled naked, leaving his garment behind. (Mark 14: 51 – 52).

These verses have nothing to do with the rest of the main story which is the arrest of Jesus. They were edited out of both Matthew and Luke and are thus unique to Mark. One theory is that this was the young John Mark who was nervously trying to follow Jesus, but it all proved too much for him and he fled. This proves nothing but the incident is all too likely to have been true, and thus this is strong evidence for the veracity of the whole passage. This principle is known by scholars as the *criterion of dissimilarity.* Another example is the mention of the four brothers of Jesus in Mark, Chapter 6, verse 3. They are stated to be James, Joseph, Judas and Simon. James also appears in the Acts of the Apostles, Paul's Epistle to the Galations and the writings of Josephus. Josephus (37 CE – 100 CE) was a Jewish historian, who defected to the Romans in 67 CE, and who wrote a detailed history of the Jews in his *"Antiquities of the Jews"*. We shall come across Josephus again in more detail in Chapter 5.

Also, if a story were made up, the writer would make sure that the story was relevant to the text and thoroughly believable. One example of this is that all four Gospels describe that the first people to come to the empty tomb on the first Easter Sunday were either a woman, Mary Magdalene or one or two other women. If this story were apocryphal, then the writer would surely have had men discovering the tomb. Women were thought to be notoriously unreliable in those days and therefore in a made up story you would make sure that a man or some men discovered the tomb; otherwise no-one would believe it. Although the details differ from Gospel to Gospel, the story is thus very likely to be true. I shall return to this event in Chapter 7. This again is no proof but, in my view, very strong evidence. In the subsequent chapters, we shall make frequent reference to the New Testament, but, as we shall see, there will be some verses that will cause surprise.

Finally, mention should be made of the Dead Sea Scrolls. In December 1945, a young Bedouin shepherd boy idly tossed a stone into a cave and heard it strike and break what appeared to be pot. This happened in the Qumran area near the Dead Sea. He and his friends investigated further and discovered a large number of clay jars containing rolled up scrolls, that had been hidden away there presumably for safe keeping. This was an amazing archaeological find, for during the next ten years, until 1956, archaeologists discovered some 961 different texts in a mass of jars, which had lain there forgotten for centuries in a series of caves. Partial or complete copies of all the books in the Old Testament were discovered with the curious exception of the book of Esther. (Well, I did state earlier in this chapter that Esther is one of only two books in the Bible not to mention God). There is a lot about a group of people called the Essenes, who lived and flourished in the area in the two centuries just before Jesus. At the time this was thought to be a huge sensation and everyone involved hoped that sooner or later some hidden texts about Jesus would be unearthed. Sadly, this was not to be and there was no scroll that made any reference to Jesus.

Chapter 3:
The Next World.

In this chapter we are going to examine what I believe is going to happen to us once we die. Is there a life after this one? If so, is there any evidence about where we go and what our existence is likely to be? Let's be honest here: this is the BIG QUESTION that nearly all of us think about especially once we start to grow older. This is a subject that the Christian Church used to say a great deal about, but curiously, the Church seems to be much less forthcoming in recent times. It is also reasonable to ask where we were, if anywhere, before we came into this world. Nihilists, or those who reject all religious principles, believe that we come from nowhere and we are going nowhere. In fact many of us, without much idea of who we really are, move between the two great mysteries of where we came from and where we are going to go – if anywhere, without being too bothered. For these people, once this life is over, it's good-bye and that's that. They might argue that the process of dying could be akin to undergoing a general anaesthetic: at one stage, one is fully conscious, then comes the rather "woosy" pre-med and then finally absolutely nothing, which they might argue is by definition no problem. A further point that they could put forward is that if nothing else, then at least one lives on in the memories of those who are left behind. Furthermore, if one happens to have children, then there is an additional genetic legacy. Despite all this and interestingly, there has been some recent research in the United

States of America, which shows that whereas the number of believers in God is actually going down, the number of people who believe in some sort of afterlife has actually gone up from 73% in 1972 to 80% in 2014. Furthermore, a British survey by the Institute of Education in London in 2012 found that about half of Britons believe in some form of afterlife while only about one third have any belief in God. In this chapter, we are going to examine what evidence, if any, there might be for a life after this one, and then, if there is such an existence, in the next chapter, we will see how God might fit into this scenario.

I believe that each one of us has three parts: body, mind and spirit or soul. At death, the body is discarded. It has served its purpose and it rots away, or it is cremated. The mind is closely connected to the soul, and I hope very much that at least in part, the mind continues its existence. It is the soul that moves on into its new life.

A few years ago, my wife and I attended a funeral of an elderly lady whom we can call Mary. She was the proud matriarch of a family of three children and several grandchildren most of whom were already grown up. She had been much loved by all her family, had lived a full life, but now at an advanced age, it was time for her to move on. She had a firm faith all her life and one had the impression that Mary in true character would have been watching in on the funeral and taking a good interest in everything that was going on. At one stage the vicar who was taking the service, said something which I had never heard before or since at a funeral: he said "We are all probably wondering, 'Where is Mary now?'" It was a good question and very relevant. The idea that Mary might be totally extinguished and non-existent was unthinkable. But where was she? The short answer was that no-one knew, including the vicar himself. It is my belief that Mary was very much around, and, at the time of her funeral, perhaps not too far away, keeping a close and interested watch on proceedings, and noting who was present. But she was in a different plane or dimension. Funerals are very important. If done correctly and with due feeling, they can and should be a great source of comfort to the bereaved, and, in my opinion, very likely also to the recently departed who may well be present at the funeral in spirit. Interestingly, more and more people are opting for a service of celebration of the life of the departed, especially if that life has been a long and full one.

Is there any direct evidence that life goes on after this one? My answer to this question is a very firm "YES". I believe that even people who have no belief in an afterlife will find themselves somewhere in another existence – often to their amazement. For example, there are a large number of people who have been through a Near Death Experience (N.D.E.). Over the past 50 or so years, there have been an ever increasing number of people who have recorded this experience. An N.D.E. has been known to happen in the operating theatre when a difficult life or death operation is taking place and the patient "dies" for a few minutes. This means that the heart stops beating and there is little or no activity from the brain. In the past, that would have meant the patient died. In more recent years with the advance of medical expertise and resuscitation, it has often been possible for the patient to return to a more or less normal life. It is what the patient then reports that can be truly amazing and interesting. Each case varies in detail but there is often a common theme. Frequently a patient reports that they have been floating in the air near the ceiling of the operating theatre and looking down at what is going on, while the surgeons are working frantically to revive a lifeless body on the operating theatre bed. This means that they see their own body. Also, they are sometimes in a position to see other things in the room that would otherwise be obscured, such as an article lying on top of a cupboard that no-one at ground level would see. The details will vary but this is the sort of report that a number of people have given after an N.D.E.

In other cases, patients record that they feel they are floating in the air, and then moving or falling through a long dark tunnel. At the end of the tunnel, there is usually a bright light, at which point, it seems that many people come up to a barrier which I will call the "Point Of No Return". It is then that the "traveller" might meet up with one or more "dead" relatives who often appear to be in their prime. At this stage the relatives, although showing great love, say something like, "Go Back! It's not time for you to come over". Or it might be: "You still have work to do on Earth." Sometimes it is an encounter with a Supreme Being of Light or a very Bright Light from which a voice comes saying much the same thing. Other people enjoy a glimpse into the next world and talk of its extreme peace and beauty. Understandably, the traveller is reluctant to go back. Why re-enter a painful and diseased human body when all seems so blissful and pain free? But some do return and suddenly re-enter their earthly body, much to the delight of those on earth who have been fighting for them. Those who do return then have a remarkable tale to record, and often the remainder of their earthly life is quite transformed because they have "seen the Light". The experiences can be summed up as some or all of the following:

1. A sense of floating above one's body.

2. A feeling of detachment.

3. Complete peace and painlessness; the body feels fit and strong and in its prime.

4. Drifting or falling through a tunnel.

5. Encountering loved ones who have died.

6. Encountering a Supreme Being of Light.

7. Extreme reluctance to return to the earthly body.

8. Greater calm and peace on returning to this life, and the patient often feels much better, as if they have been healed.

9. No fear of death when it comes, perhaps some years later.

It is easy to dismiss this as hallucination and in some cases it may be just that. But it is difficult to say that all N.D.E. experiences are hallucination. It is noteworthy that if the patient has been under the influence of strong drugs during their illness, the chances of an N.D.E. are less, rather than more. Also, the experiences of people who have been blind from birth, or soon after birth, are interesting because it appears that they are able to "see" perfectly well during their N.D.E. and are able to give vivid descriptions. There are many books that have been written describing an N.D.E. experience and the reader who is interested in this fascinating subject is encouraged to read further. A good example is *"Dying to be me"* by Anita Moorjani. This book describes how an Indian woman who was brought up as a Hindu, comes back from being very close to death from a vicious cancer. She returns to this life and very soon is completely cured of the cancer.

For our purposes, it is sufficient to say that there is a lot of evidence now that there is a process that does seem to happen at the time that a person "passes over". Furthermore, it does not seem to matter whether the person involved has or has not a religious faith. This could just as well happen to a Christian, a Muslim, a Jew, an agnostic or atheist, or any other religion. This could be upsetting to those who believe that we can only secure an afterlife by having the correct religious faith. But I see no reason for this to interfere with a strongly held religious faith.

There is another area where there does seem to be something going on "over there", and that is when we examine the subject of ghosts. The whole subject tends to be avoided by many people, because it is all rather creepy, disturbing and downright scary. However, ghosts have appeared throughout history. In the Bible there is reference to a ghost during the Resurrection story when the disciples first encounter Jesus:

They were startled and frightened thinking they saw a ghost. (Luke 24: 37).

This was the first occasion when many of the disciples encountered the resurrected Jesus and no wonder they were startled and frightened.

Ghosts also appear throughout history in many stories including in Shakespeare's *"Macbeth"* and *"Hamlet"*. But there are also numerous occasions in real life when they have appeared in old houses and generally have scared the wits out of occupants who were not prepared for the encounter.

So what are ghosts? Are they real or are they the product of a vivid imagination of sensitive people, in other words, hallucinations? Well, probably many reported cases are hallucinations but there are so many well researched and credible cases, that it is difficult to dismiss all reports that way. There are plenty of cases where perfectly sensible down to earth, rational and unexcitable people have encountered some form of ghost. Indeed, I have direct experience of a *poltergeist*, a German word meaning "noisy ghost". Usually, no actual ghost is seen but the evidence is real enough with, for example, lights turned on, noises created and things moved around. A poltergeist experience often turns out to be far more creepy then the appearance of an actual ghost. It is my belief that this is the result of a spirit being trapped at some lower level in the next world, and, being by nature mischievous, it creates trouble in this world. In my own case, this was what we found in our Channel Island home when we returned there in 1945 after the World War II Occupation. We do not know quite what went on during the war, but the house was commandeered by German soldiers. My mother found a *planchette* which is a small board on castors, with a pencil, said to trace messages from the spirit world. She immediately threw it away. It seems likely that séances took place in the house and perhaps there was a tragedy. Anyway, it soon became apparent that some spirit was trapped there. Lights and taps were turned on and bells were heard to ring, although there was not a bell in the house. This was downright scary for a small child. The situation gradually got worse, and there was a definite tension in the house. In the end my parents decided to send for the local Roman Catholic priest to come and deal with the situation, having decided that this would be beyond the powers of the well-meaning but rather elderly Church of England Rector! The Catholic priest arrived, sprinkled some holy water around the place, and in a prayer, asked the spirit in effect to move on. Fortunately this worked and life happily returned to normal. Why do I record this? The answer is that it was all too real, and, for my younger brother and me, a nightmare. But I interpret this to be direct evidence of a spirit trapped at some lowly level in the next world. This spirit was not necessarily evil, but just mischievous. I believe that this is the explanation for many reported sightings of ghosts and poltergeists. There are simply too many reliable people who have reported encounters with ghosts or spirits, for this to be unbelievable. They are spirits that have passed over but for some reason have got stuck at some lowly or intermediate stage. In some cases they may not even have realised that they have died. In a meaningful way, they really are lost souls. At an exorcism, it should be possible to encourage these souls to pull themselves together and move on.

It is my firm belief that some of our loved ones who have passed on, are watching us at least some of the time, and perhaps even trying to guide us. This may be a dead spouse, sibling, parent or grandparent – or even just a friend. When we do pass over and get beyond the Point of No Return, we are usually first met by a loved one. So what happens to a loner – someone who has no immediate family available? Well, there will be someone or some kind soul who will help out. I believe that it could even be possible for a person to be first greeted by, say, a faithful dog that has already passed over. I shall return to this theme in the section on animals in Chapter 11. Others watching over us may not be known directly to us, but they can be looked upon as Guardian Angels. The Roman Catholic and Russian Orthodox Churches believe strongly in the idea of a Guardian Angel. Angels are very prominent in the Bible, both the Old Testament and the New Testament. An early example in the Old Testament is when the angel of the Lord appears to Abraham when he is about to slay his son, Isaac, as a sacrifice:

Then he (Abraham) *reached out his hand and took out the knife to slay his son. But the angel of the Lord called out to him from heaven, "Abraham! Abraham!" "Here I am," he replied. "Do not lay a hand on the boy," he said. "Do not do anything to him. Now that I know that you fear God, because you have not withheld from me your son, your only son."* (Genesis 22: 10 - 12).

There are also examples in the New Testament when the angel of the Lord appears to Joseph encouraging him to take his wife Mary and the baby Jesus and flee to Egypt, as shown in Matthew Chapter 2 verse 13. Later on in the Acts of the Apostles, the Angel of the Lord appears to Peter and John, and also Paul. A dramatic example comes in the Acts of the Apostles when Peter is in prison:

The night before Herod was to bring him to trial, Peter was sleeping between two soldiers, bound with two chains, and sentries stood guard at the entrance. Suddenly an angel of the Lord appeared and a light shone in the cell. He struck Peter on the side and woke him up. "Quick, get up!" he said, and the chains fell off Peter's wrists. Then the angel said to him, "Put on your clothes and sandals." And Peter did so. "Wrap your cloak around you and follow me," the angel told him. (Acts 12: 6 – 8).

The passage then goes on to describe how the Angel of the Lord then led a bewildered Peter out of the prison past various guards. All this indicates that at least in Biblical times, people really did believe in angels existing outside this world.

I cannot prove it, but I hope this chapter will show that there is a lot of evidence that there is an existence beyond our space and time. As long as we are in this world, we will never be sure exactly what happens to the soul after we die, but it is my belief that we reach and pass through the Point Of No Return as described earlier. After that? Well, I suggest three possible scenarios:

1.   If the person has died very suddenly, then the soul may well be in need of a period of readjustment because it may not even realise what has happened. It may need help just to realise that the person has passed over and is no longer alive on earth.

2.   A period of complete rest if the person has endured a long and painful final illness.

3.   After scenarios 1 or 2, the soul may then be in a position to review its past life from a position of unconditional and divine love. This will be very painful for anyone who has led a particularly evil life.

I have never claimed to be in any way psychic, but there have been occasions in my life when I have had the most vivid dreams about someone soon after his or her death. As a rule, they appear somewhat younger than they were in their final years on earth. Generally the message is one of great joy and contentment.   Just one example of this concerns a rather outspoken Yorkshireman with whom I used to work closely and who died suddenly in a tragic accident while riding his bicycle. He was a great railway enthusiast, and in my dream, he was standing at a station and beaming broadly. In the dream I got a firm message from him: "Eee lad, you were a great mate!" Wherever he was, he seemed fine and very happy with his new life.

The Bible has some very relevant comments about the next world. For example:

"In my father's house are many rooms, if it were not so, I would have told you." (John 14: 2).

The Revised Version of the Bible uses the word *"mansions"* in place of *"rooms"*. I prefer the word *"mansions"*, but that is by the way. The point is that after a period of adjustment and if necessary rest, as described in my three possible scenarios above, we move on to some "mansion" but there are a huge number of them and they are all at very different levels depending upon how advanced we are as a soul. After that, well, who knows but it will be fascinating to see, but at least we can believe most firmly that something happens and we do not end up in oblivion. The Christian Church teaches that in order to have eternal life, we need to repent and believe in God, Jesus Christ and his Resurrection. There are many people in this world who lead a very worthy and Christian life without actually being believers even in an afterlife. They care passionately for their families and do their utmost to relieve any suffering in this world. It is my firm belief that such people are in for a very pleasant surprise once they die. They will find that there is a life after this one and a lot will start to be revealed to them. This implies that those that have led a good Christian life can reasonably hope to move to a "mansion" at a reasonably higher level.

At the start of this chapter I also asked whether we have any existence before this life. This question is actually the more difficult one to answer, but it is a good question. My own belief is that many of us would have had such an existence, but it is not easy to provide any direct evidence of this. This belief would tie in with Hinduism which we will look at in Chapter 9. However, the Bible does have two curious verses on this subject when the prophet Jeremiah claims a previous existence:

The word of the Lord came to me saying, "Before I formed you in the womb, I knew you, before you were born I set you apart; I appointed you as a prophet to the nations." (Jeremiah 1: 4-5).

The sceptic might reasonably argue that this is just wishful thinking on Jeremiah's part, and we must leave it at that for the time being. I shall refer to this topic again in Chapter 12.

There are still many who believe in a medieval Heaven and Hell. Some people might think of Heaven as a place that the righteous can aspire to after this life, a place of bliss in the sky and the abode of God. Likewise, Hell has been thought of as a place of eternal torment. In a nutshell, have a good life on Earth and you will go to Heaven, otherwise it's off to Hell and misery. I do not believe that it is as simple as that, nor do I believe in the Devil or Satan. Hell is a very negative idea, and suggesting that anyone who does not believe in God, will be condemned to Hell is so counterproductive. All it does is bring in a degree of spiritual tension that is not going to help anyone. There are many levels in the Next World, and yes, the very lowest level might be quite uncomfortable and gloomy, but it is not Hell in the accepted sense, and I see no reason why anyone would need to stay there for ever. If Hell exists at all, it could be during the process of thinking about one's past life, and then realising how much better it could have been. This could indeed feel very unpleasant to say the least. There can also be a feeling of Hell on earth: I can well remember one clear occasion in London when a certain Bishop got caught in the London traffic. He finally arrived considerably late for the engagement, and thundered into the room: "If ever there is Hell on earth, I have just been through it!" Likewise, Heaven is not a matter of sitting idly on a cloud and playing a harp. How boring would that be after a time! I do accept that there are higher levels in the next world that could feel quite heavenly, but that does not mean to say that one would be there to sit still.

There is one final thought on the subject of an existence after this one. As I indicated earlier, it is after all the BIG QUESTION that all humans must think about especially as they start to grow older, even if they do not admit to it. There are some who may think that if there is an existence after this one with some form of Final Judgment, well, it might be best not to behave too badly while on Earth, just in case. For myself, if I were ever persuaded that there was not a life after this one, *I would not alter my behaviour in this life at all.* After all, there must still surely be a Supreme Goodness behind it all.

There is a further question that could be asked: the Christian faith teaches that there is a life after this one for all who believe. Should this be a matter of great comfort? For Christians, and indeed, other religions, this should surely be the case. And yet the position is not quite as simple. A recent survey suggests that those who have no belief in an afterlife are more content than some who do have such a belief. The idea is that if there is no afterlife, it's oblivion, that's it and by definition, no problem. On the other hand, if there is an afterlife, it might not be too comfortable and therefore a degree of uncertainty and discomfort might creep in. From my own point of view, I see no reason to be anxious.

In conclusion, the final message of this chapter is that *there is a life after this one,* albeit probably very different from the Heaven or Hell ideas put forth by some parts of the Christian Church, and indeed other religions.

Chapter 4:
Why I believe in God

This is another BIG QUESTION. Does one believe in God, and if so, what sort of God is he? The existence of God is arguably the single most important question we face about the nature of reality. Is it possible to have a life after this one and yet have no God? Curiously, there are many people who think that this could be the case, as I have shown in the previous chapter, but I really cannot go along with that.

To my mind, if we do have a life after this one, there has to be some Supreme Organiser behind it all, and that Organiser is completely benign. I cannot prove the existence of God in the way that I can prove, for example, the mathematical theorem of Pythagoras. Equally, there can be no reasonable proof that God does *not* exist. St Thomas Aquinas (1225 – 1274) was born in the 13th century in Roccasecca, Italy. In his time, he was an immensely influential philosopher and theologian, and he produced five "proofs" for the existence of God. The first four are all rather too philosophical for us to get involved with, but the fifth "proof" stated that all bodies in nature followed natural laws and that everything flowed in a natural order.

Besides our Faith in God, there are a number of good reasons that can be put forward for the existence of God. Straightaway, we can consider miracles and, in particular, the Resurrection which we will come on to in Chapter 7. Miracles contradict the known laws of nature and thus one way to explain them is to accept that there is a Divine Power behind them that allows the miracles to happen. There are plenty of miracle stories in the Gospels and, indeed, elsewhere in the Bible. Then throughout history, there have been healing miracles, or, at any rate, what have been taken to be miracles. There will be more on this in the later chapters on Jesus.

Further strong evidence for the existence of God that I find to be powerful can come from an appreciation of science. Again this is no proof but if one goes outside on a dark evening in the countryside well away from urban lights, it is possible to see the full magnificence of the heavens. There are stars to be seen everywhere, some bright, some faint and mostly very very distant - that is many light years away. Could this all be by chance? The more we understand about physics, the more we can see that the universe turns out to be very finely tuned. One example is the mass of an electron, a constant in nature. If this had been only slightly different, stars could not have formed in the way that they did. The same applies to other constants in nature such as the speed of light, the gravitational force and the electromagnetic force. Even the orbit of the Earth is just in the right position and distance from the Sun, this being called a "Goldilocks" orbit. If the Earth had evolved even slightly closer to the Sun, it would have become like Venus is to-day which has suffered a run-away greenhouse effect, far too hot with a thick carbon dioxide atmosphere, and quite impossible for life to evolve. If the Earth had evolved outside the Goldilocks orbit, it would have frozen hard and become much too cold. As it turns out, the Earth is just the right distance from the Sun to be about a reasonable temperature. The Moon also has played a vital role for us to evolve. It happens that the Moon is relatively large compared with the Earth, its diameter being about one quarter of that of the Earth. This is most unusual for a small planet to have such a large moon. It probably came about because a planet about the size of Mars collided with the Earth very early on. Then a chunk of the Earth was ejected into space, where at first it formed rings like the ones around the planet Saturn. These rings then coalesced into the body we now call the Moon. The Moon stabilized the rate of the Earth's spin so that we have a fairly long day. It also stabilized the angle of the Earth's axis to give us regular seasons and prevent the extremes of temperature. Although this is all rather technical, I simply ask to reader to accept that everything is all exactly right, for the universe and in particular the Earth for life to evolve, and the more one is able to delve into this subject, the more remarkable it all becomes. The more science looks into this topic, the more evident it is that the whole universe is very finely tuned, otherwise it could not have come into being. What matters is that the Earth was able to acquire plenty of water, essential for life (although how that came about is still hotly debated), and the Earth was just the right size and in the right position for life to evolve. There has been plenty of time for this to have come about. Science now tells us that the Earth, our Solar System and the Sun are some 4.56 billion years old. But this is not the age of the universe, which is now thought to be about 13.8 billion years old, when the so called "Big Bang" started the whole process off. In passing it is worth noting that the ages of the Earth and the Sun turn out to be around just one third of the age of the Universe. Quite how the Universe happened, quite how it all came about, how much God was involved in it all - let's be honest about this – no one has the faintest idea. Nor have we any idea of what if anything was around before the Big Bang. In this topic, words must fail and the mind boggles. Let's just accept that God probably had a lot to do with the creation of the Universe, it's beyond our comprehension and leave it at that.

The other relevant question at this stage is: Is life on Earth unique in our universe? Or quite simply: ARE WE ALONE? We do not know the answer to this question, but it is absolutely fundamental to our religious beliefs. One day, we may find evidence of some form of life elsewhere and that is going to have a profound effect on both science and theology.

For years scientists have wondered whether there is life elsewhere in the Solar System. Is there, or was there ever, life on Mars, which is the next planet away from the Sun away from the Earth? Mars is a relatively small planet, just over half the diameter of the Earth, and is outside the "Goldilocks" area, but not that far from it. With the advance of space exploration, we can now be sure that water did once flow freely on the early Mars. Scientists now strongly suspect that there is water in liquid form below the surface of Mars. It is just possible that primitive life might have once started there, but in Patrick Moore's words, there are no "Bug Eyed Monsters". The planet is simply too cold and to-day it is a frigid, dried up desert. However, it is the one planet, that, with advancing technology, man might one day be able to live on. Another remote possibility for life is Europa, one of the large moons of Jupiter, that is about the size of our own Moon. Europa we now know is covered by a huge ice sheet underneath which, there is probably a large ocean of water.

Another possibility that has recently been in the news is the much smaller moon named Enceladus that circles the planet Saturn. This also seems to be covered in ice or snow and appears very bright and white, with liquid water below the surface. Is there primitive life living in these oceans in the way that life has evolved in underwater seas beneath Antarctica? As yet we do not know the answer. We can, however, be sure that there is no advanced civilization in our Solar System.

What about planets around other stars? In recent years thousands of planets have been discovered around some of the closer stars. Most of the planets that have been discovered so far are either much too large like our Jupiter or they are curiously much too close to the star. Recent discoveries have found, however, that there are indeed earth sized planets inside the "Goldilocks" zone of other stars. They may well be habitable planets but there is a huge difference between a planet that is habitable, and one that is actually inhabited. Could life and even intelligent life have evolved in any of these planets? It seems that given these worlds are so far away, it will be a very long time, if ever, before we know the answer. However, given the huge number of planets that there must be throughout the universe and not only in our Milky Way galaxy, it seems highly likely that there could be a considerable number of planets of the right size within the "Goldilocks" area, where the conditions for life of some sort to form would be just right. The problem is that we still have no real idea as to how life started on this Earth. Was it some magical chemical chance or did God have a hand in it all?

It is necessary at this stage to examine the process of evolution and the arguments of Richard Dawkins, the well-known atheist. Dawkins is a remarkable man who sprang to fame with his book, *The Selfish Gene,* published in 1976. He has since written a number of other best-selling books, in which he maintains that God is not necessary for the universe to come into being and for life to form on this planet. Whether one agrees or disagrees with Dawkins, there is no doubt that he is a gifted communicator. What some of his books do explain is how evolution has come about by quite natural means. Furthermore, he explains it all very clearly, and I have no problem with any of that. Where I part company with him is that he argues that because evolution can be shown to happen without Divine intervention, then there is no need for God and therefore God does not exist. My argument is that evolution neither proves nor disproves the existence of God. It must surely be perfectly possible for evolution to exist as Dawkins describes *and for this to be God's creative work.*

There are still other factors that can be put forward for the existence of a totally Benign Organiser. One is the exquisite beauty and scent of some flowers in nature. We can also add in the beauty of some of the animals on earth, and many of the natural surroundings. In fact I believe that God and his angels look upon this world as one of very great beauty. Thus it pains me greatly when we destroy natural habitats purely for greedy gain.

Another factor is the strong sense of moral values that so many of us have. There are also so many people who have prayers that have been answered, at least to their own satisfaction. Finally, I sometimes find God most powerfully in certain people. From time to time, I feel privileged to meet certain people, perhaps one in a hundred, who are what I call *"Advanced Humans"* or *"Advanced Souls"*. They are wonderful and very loving human beings, not necessarily saints at all, but from whom the spirit of God shines forth so brilliantly. The love of one human being for another in its many possible forms is so important and is yet another manifestation of God. I shall return to this theme in my final chapter. Again, none of these is a proof of God, but, cumulatively, these factors must all add up to something.

Summary: I suggest that there are three possible scenarios:

1. The first is that everything came about accidentally. But the odds of this happening are so minute that no scientist to-day can readily accept it. This is the equivalent of throwing six after six after six in a game of dice billions of times. It just does not happen!

2. A second possibility is that this universe is just one amongst a huge number of universes or a "multiverse". The idea is that is you have enough universes, then one of them will happen to strike lucky and get all the fundamental constants just right. It has been estimated that it would be necessary to have 10^{500} (1 followed by 500 noughts!) universes for there to be one that was just right for life to evolve. But we are into fantasy land here. Even light cannot travel from one "side" of

our universe to the other "side" in the time since the universe has existed, and nothing can travel faster than light. So another universe is a purely theoretical concept. The problem is that there is no way that we could ever communicate with another universe, let alone ever find any evidence that such a universe could even exist. The whole idea is just too far-fetched (literally!) to have any reasonable credibility at all.

3.   The third scenario is that there is a Supreme Organiser behind all of this. Again, I emphasise that this does not prove the existence of God, but in with my belief, it does all fit together remarkably well. We can describe the universe as a wonderful gigantic 3-dimensional jig-saw puzzle with a supreme interaction between all the pieces. *Surely only God could have constructed such a universe.*

So what about it? God may be often portrayed as some kind of old man with a long flowing white beard sitting on a cloud somehow directing the Universe. But no, he is everywhere as a totally Benign and Omnipotent Presence. He is a God for everyone, whether they are believers or not. I do not believe in a God who consigns people to Hell and damnation for not accepting God or Jesus. What we have to do is to find God. Then we have to realise that God is infinitely kind, good and forgiving. If there is one parable in the Gospels that describes God clearly, it is the parable of the Prodigal Son where God is the father as we shall see in Chapter 6. The message from this all important chapter is that behind everything, I believe very firmly that *there is a Benign Creator.*

Chapter 5:
Jesus 1: His
Conception and Birth.

In this and the following two chapters we will examine in some detail the life of Jesus Christ. There are three questions that I am going to try to answer:

1. Did he exist and, if so, who was he?

2. Was he some part of God, and if so, was he the Son of God?

3. Or was he an exceptional human being chosen to act as a prophet, like Mohammad?

One thing we can establish quite quickly and easily: his human existence is undeniable. It is true that some have tried to argue that Jesus was merely a figment of the imagination of St Paul. It is also true that there are some people, called mythicists, who take the view that the whole thing is pure myth - Jesus, the disciples and Paul himself. But there is plenty of evidence of Jesus the man both in the Bible and in writings outside the Bible. Nearly every scholar would to-day agree that Jesus was a Jewish man, who was a great teacher and who was crucified sometime around the year 30 or 33 CE when Pontius Pilate was the governor of Judea, and Tiberius was the Roman emperor. Even atheists and agnostics generally accept that Jesus existed and was crucified. Not only do we have the evidence of the four Gospels in the Bible, but we also have frequent references to him by Paul in the Pauline Epistles and the rest of the New Testament. There is also reference to him in external sources. The chief of these is the Jewish historian Josephus, who was born about 37 or 38 CE, the son of a Judean priest. In 66 CE he helped to defend Galilee against the Romans during the Jewish revolt. However, he was captured and deciding that resistance was useless, he defected to the Romans. He moved to Rome where he was well regarded, and he had time and leisure to write *The Jewish War* about 77 CE. Towards the end of the first century he wrote his Magnum Opus *The Antiquities of the Jews.* The important thing about Josephus is that he is well respected by historians because of his attention to detail making it possible to verify much of what he wrote using archaeological techniques. He was not a Christian, but he was interested in religion and he does seem to have been at pains to be accurate and objective. He does indeed mention Jesus in *Antiquities,* though only briefly, writing:

At about this time lived Jesus, a wise man.....

I have not reproduced the rest of the passage which may have been clumsily adulterated by a pro-Christian group, but the above sentence rings true. Later in *Antiquities*, there is reference to James, who was supposed to be Jesus' brother. Josephus refers to the unjust execution in 62 CE of James "*the brother of Jesus called the Christ*". The Roman historian, Tacitus, also makes a brief reference to Christians whose originator "*Christ had been executed in Tiberius' reign.*" Furthermore, the Qur'an has plenty to say about Jesus as a man, and indeed a very good man, one of the prophets. Few people would deny that there was such a man. But often the view is expressed that yes, Jesus existed, he was a great teacher and an admirable example and yes, there were times when he had the amazing ability to make people feel a lot better, but the Son of God, no way. In this and the following two chapters, I shall attempt to show that he was indeed the Son of God.

Before we go any further, we need to draw a distinction between the *Jesus of Faith* and the *Jesus of History*. If we wish to stick with the Jesus of Faith, and accept all the stories in the Gospels at face value, then that is fine, and we can proceed perfectly well along that path. This is the Jesus that was later perceived and understood by the Church. After all, if God is omnipotent, then he can control the laws of nature and miracles can perfectly well happen. But if, on the other hand, we are prepared to at least look at the Jesus of History, then be prepared! It is not such an easy path. *And it is on this point that there have been so many dissensions and difficulties within the Christian Church.* On one side there are those of a more Evangelical belief who take everything about Jesus in the Bible as literally true while on the other side there are those who take a more thoughtful and critical approach. This second group includes most of those who are academics and theologians. Furthermore, these divergences apply to the whole Bible, including, in particular the Old Testament. What we are talking about is how we bring faith and reason together. One of the aims of this book is to show that this is perfectly possible. To the Jesus of Faith and the Jesus of History, we could also add the *Jesus of Mystery.* There are some things about Jesus that are, at present, just beyond our understanding.

At this stage, I am going to concentrate upon the Jesus of History. This is the Jesus who lived and worked in Palestine and who was crucified on the Cross. There are many historians who study the gospels and other evidence and then decide that miracles, for example, just do not and did not happen. In their view, the miracles in the gospels are pure myth – these are stories that have built up around the cult of Jesus. These historians would take the same view about the Virgin Birth and the Resurrection. *Nevertheless, I firmly believe that a study of the Jesus of History does not and **should not** lead to a loss of faith.* In my own case, it has rather led to a more thoughtful, intelligent and stronger faith. To elaborate this point a little further: in Chapter 2, I pointed out that John's Gospel is radically different to the three synoptic Gospels, Matthew, Mark and Luke. John's Gospel contains the great "*I am*" statements, such as "*I am the way and the truth and the life,*" "*I am the true vine,*" and "*I am the light of the world*". John's Gospel also contains the famous verse:

"*For God so loved the world that he gave his one and only son, that whoever believes in him shall not perish but have eternal life.*" (John 3: 16).

These verses are not found anywhere within the Synoptics. Many scholars now consider John's Gospel to contain many of the Jesus of Faith verses that were not true historically, but nevertheless have tremendous meaning. Thus they were added by the Christian church after the death of Jesus some 60 or so years later. Many of the verses in John's Gospel were written down by the writer as being sayings that they thought Jesus might have said. By contrast, if we want to examine the Jesus of History, we would do well to begin with Mark's Gospel, which shows Jesus in a far more human and down to earth person.

****

In this chapter, we shall examine the Virgin Birth; in Chapter 6, we shall examine the life of Jesus, including the miracles and in Chapter 7, we shall examine the all-important topic of the Resurrection. The aim will be to see whether we can bring the idea of the Jesus of Faith closer to the Jesus of History. In other words, we are going to ask, *"What really happened?"*

The Christian teaching has always been that Jesus' mother, Mary, was a virgin at the time of his birth, and that Joseph was not Jesus' biological father. Whatever the position this must not be confused with the "Immaculate Conception" which is a Roman Catholic dogma about the conception of Mary. Roman Catholics believe that Mary herself was immaculately conceived and was free from sin throughout her life. This is the doctrine of the Perpetual Virginity of Mary which goes back to the fourth century CE. There is no evidence for this anywhere in the Bible but it is a belief that grew up strongly in later years.

Now the dogma of Virgin Birth or rather the Virgin Conception is a tough one to sell. A young unmarried girl called Mary, probably a teenager, somehow gets pregnant, but the father is not a man, but rather some miracle arranged by God. Some Christians, such as the Roman Catholics mentioned above, also believe that Mary remained a virgin even after the birth of a strapping baby boy. This is the story of the Virgin Birth, believed and beloved by every branch of the Christian faith. Yet, to many theologians, this sounds so incredible, that they reject it and this is not the Jesus of History. In fact I have found that many historians try to duck this one altogether. They do not believe in it and prefer not to discuss it with those who have faith. And yet for many Christians this one is a deal-breaker. Some might argue that you can have doubts about, for example, the miracle of turning water into wine, but the Virgin Birth is sacrosanct, and without it Christianity falls apart. We shall now examine carefully what evidence there is and also whether this really is that important.

We shall start by examining Mark's Gospel:

When the Sabbath came, he (Jesus) *began to teach in the synagogue, and many who heard him were amazed. "Where did this man get these things?" they asked. "What's this wisdom that has been given him, that he even does miracles! Isn't this the carpenter? Isn't this Mary's son and the brother of James, Joseph, Judas and Simon? Aren't his sisters here with us?" And they took offence at him.* (Mark 6: 2 - 3)

Matthew's Gospel says much the same thing:

Coming to his home town, he (Jesus) *began teaching the people in their synagogue, and they were amazed. "Where did this man get his wisdom and these miraculous powers?" they asked. "Isn't this the carpenter's son? Isn't his mother's name Mary, and aren't his brothers James, Joseph, Simon and Judas? Aren't all his sisters with us? Where did this man get all these things?" And they took offence at him.* (Matt. 13: 54 – 57).

Notice two small differences: the order of the final two brothers has been reversed in Matthew's version. But more significantly, where Mark has "Isn't this the carpenter?" Matthew has "Isn't this the *carpenter's son?*" (Incidentally, this is the only reference in the whole of the Bible that Jesus was a carpenter). Thus Matthew's version implies that Jesus did have an earthly father, presumably Joseph. Both these gospels imply that Jesus had four brothers who are named, and at least two sisters, who are not named. Thus the implication is that even if Mary had been a virgin at the time of Jesus' birth, she did not remain one after the birth of at least a further six children, fathered presumably by Joseph.

We have already come across James in the writings of Josephus and he is mentioned again in The Acts of the Apostles (Acts 12: 17), Paul's first Epistle to the Corinthians (I Cor. 15: 7) and Paul's Epistle to the Galatians (Gal. 1: 19). In this last case, Paul actually writes *"James, the Lord's brother"*. As I mentioned in Chapter 2, the Epistle of James in the New Testament, may well have been written by this James, the brother of Jesus. This Epistle is full of simple down to earth pieces of practical advice, that could have come straight from the mouth of Jesus himself. Thus there is plenty of evidence that Jesus had a brother named James. Also, Judas may have been the Jude who wrote the very short Epistle that is the penultimate book of the Bible. As I have said, there are some Christians who are determined that Mary remained a virgin and they try to get round this conundrum by suggesting that the brothers and sisters were Joseph's children from a previous marriage. We need to examine this idea carefully. In the early Christian era, there built up a very strong tradition about Mary that she remained a virgin all her life. Thus the non-Canonical Infancy "Gospel" of James was written. To get round the difficulty of Jesus having brothers and sisters, this "Gospel" makes the claim that they were indeed the children of Joseph by an earlier marriage. Furthermore, Joseph is portrayed as being quite elderly by the time of the birth of Jesus. Thus James, Joseph, Judas and Simon and the sisters were Jesus' step-siblings. To me, this idea is just too fanciful and there is not a shred of evidence for it anywhere else. It would incidentally mean that James, the presumed eldest of Jesus' brothers would have to have been born around 15 BCE or probably even earlier, which would make him approaching 80 when he was executed in 62 CE. The Bible implies that Mary had at least six more children and it is very reasonable to assume that Joseph was the natural father. Another view in the early church was that James, Joseph, Judas and Simon were not Jesus' brothers at all, but rather his cousins, and thus not the children of Mary or Joseph. The main trouble with this view is that the Greek word used in the New Testament literally means "male sibling". There is a different Greek word for cousin.

Further evidence comes from Mark's Gospel. A crowd had gathered and Jesus was preaching, when they thought that Jesus was going mad:

He (Jesus) *said this because they were saying, "He has an evil spirit." Then Jesus' mother and brothers arrived. Standing outside, they sent someone in to call him.* (Mark 3: 30 – 31).

This sentence very much implies that the brothers really were Jesus' full brothers and why would they be with Mary if they were not her sons?

So what do we know or think we know about the birth of Jesus? The only evidence comes in Matthew's Gospel and Luke's Gospel: Mark's Gospel does not have anything to say about the birth of Jesus. John's Gospel also does not mention the birth of Jesus either but does imply a perfectly natural birth, when Philip and Nathanael, two of the less well known disciples, first discovered Jesus:

Philip found Nathanael and told him, "We have found the one that Moses wrote about in the Law, and about whom the prophets also wrote – Jesus of Nazareth, the son of Joseph." (John 1: 45).

There is a further reference to Joseph in John's Gospel:

They (the crowd) *said, "Is this not Jesus, the son of Joseph, whose father and mother we know?"* (John 6: 42).

Nor does Paul refer to Jesus' birth in any of the Epistles. It does not seem to concern him. Thus there is no mention of the birth of Jesus anywhere in the writings of Mark, John and Paul, in fact there is no mention of a Virgin Birth anywhere in the New Testament other than in the Gospels of Matthew and Luke. If there had been a miraculous birth, then surely the early church, including Mark, John and Paul would have known about it, and spoken about it. In fact, once we are past the first two chapters of Matthew and Luke, there is no further mention of Jesus' birth anywhere in the New Testament. And at no stage does Jesus make reference to his mother being a virgin. Thus it seems clear that the Virgin Birth stories were not central to the early Christian movement, and that this idea was something that came later. I should add, however, that the non-

Canonical "Gospel" of James does make reference to a Virgin Birth, but as explained in Chapter 2, this "Gospel" is an example of folk religion, written many years later, and it should not be taken as necessarily historical.

We need now to examine the first two chapters of Matthew and Luke in some detail. As we pick out the important points in both Gospels, we notice that the two accounts are quite different and in many respects at variance with each other. Matthew begins with a genealogy of Jesus going back to Abraham. The first thing to note is that the genealogy is through Joseph, which hardly ties in with the idea of a virgin conception if Joseph had anything to do with it. Joseph's father is given as Jacob. The Luke genealogy comes in Luke Chapter 3 and is quite different:

Now Jesus himself was about thirty years old when he began his ministry. He was the son, so it was thought, of Joseph son of Heli. (Luke 3: 23).

This is odd – "*So it was thought*" – it does at least imply some doubt about the paternity of Jesus even at that time. There is hardly any further mention of Joseph in the four Gospels once Jesus is adult, apart from the occasional references given above. It is generally assumed that Joseph must have died by then. This would mean that Jesus would be head of the family, provided he was legitimate. So, Matthew has Jesus' paternal grandfather as Jacob, and Luke has the paternal grandfather as Heli. Whoever Heli was, he was not Jacob. In fact, the whole Luke genealogy which goes all the way back to Adam via David is largely different from the Matthew genealogy. All this is rather by the way, as both genealogies imply that Jesus was the son of Joseph.

So apart from the genealogies, what are the important events as given in the two gospels for the birth of Jesus? We begin with Luke's gospel which provides a simpler version of the Nativity stories. The first chapter is very long – 80 verses. Much of it concerns Elizabeth and Zacharias, who in their old age give birth to John the Baptist. Elizabeth is stated to be a relative of the Virgin Mary. Then there is the story of the Angel Gabriel appearing to the Mary and saying that she will be with child and not to be afraid. The main point here is that according to Luke, Mary was a virgin at the time of the birth of Jesus:

In the sixth month, God sent the angel Gabriel to Nazareth, a town in Galilee, to a virgin pledged to be married to a man named Joseph, a descendant of David. The virgin's name was Mary. The angel went to her and said, "Greetings, you are highly favoured! The Lord is with you." Mary was greatly troubled at his words and wondered what kind of greeting this might be. But the angel said to her, "Do not be afraid, Mary, you have found favour with God. You will be with child and give birth to a son, and you are to give him the name Jesus. He will be great and will be called the Son of the Most High. The Lord God will give him the throne of his father David, and he will reign over the house of Jacob for ever; his kingdom will never end." "How can this be," Mary asked the angel, "since I am a virgin?" The angel answered, "The Holy Spirit will come upon you, and the power of the Most High will overshadow you. So the holy one to be born will be called the Son of God." (Luke 1: 26 – 35).

In Chapter 2, Mary gives birth to her "first born", a son. There then follows the familiar stories concerning the angels, shepherds in the fields, the manger and the presentation at the temple.

There is one further reference to Joseph in Luke's Gospel. During the early part of his ministry, Jesus returned to Nazareth when he began teaching in the synagogue and all the multitudes were "amazed" at his teaching. Then we have this curious verse:

All spoke well of him and were amazed at the gracious words that came from his lips. "Isn't this Joseph's son?" they asked. (Luke 4: 22).

This sounds as if at least the crowd thought that Jesus was the son of Joseph.

The first two chapters of the Matthew Gospel are, in some ways, more interesting. Mary found that she was pregnant while she was pledged to be married to Joseph. Joseph is then described to be a righteous man and plans to divorce Mary quietly, according to Matthew 1: 18 – 19, so as not to expose her to public disgrace. This is bit strange because with or without Joseph, she is still going to have an illegitimate child. However, an angel of the Lord appears to him in a dream explaining that what has been conceived in her is from the Holy Spirit:

The virgin will be with child and will give birth to a son, and they will call him "Immanuel" which means "God with us." (Matt. 1: 23).

This is a direct quotation from the prophet Isaiah:

Therefore the Lord himself will give you a sign: The virgin will be with child and will give birth to a son, and will call him Immanuel. (Isaiah 7: 14).

All the gospels have a number of quotations from the Old Testament, but Matthew is especially prone to use them, to the extent that one cannot help wondering sometimes whether he adjusts his narrative a little too much to fit the quotations nicely.

Matthew Chapter 2 has only 23 verses but they tell two particularly interesting stories. The first concerns the Star in the East and the visit of the Magi, or the Wise Men from the East. The second story is the escape into Egypt of Joseph, Mary and the infant Jesus. The reason for this is that an angel of the Lord appears to Joseph again in a dream, (Joseph does seem to be rather good at dreaming!), and warns the small family to flee to Egypt because Herod was in a bad mood and wanted to kill Jesus, having heard about him from the Magi. Now it is a well established fact of history that Herod died in 4 BCE. This means that if this story is true, then Jesus would have had to have been born about 6 or 5 BCE. At this stage, the reader might well wonder how Jesus came to be born BCE. In the sixth century CE a monk by the name of Dionysius Exiguus tried to change the Roman method of calculating dates, and to produce a dating system where Jesus was born in 1 CE, but, unfortunately, he got his maths wrong by about 5 or 6 years, and we are stuck with the result. If we return to the flight into Egypt story, this is directly contradicted by two verses in Luke Chapter 2:

When the time of their purification according to the law of Moses had been completed, Joseph and Mary took him to Jerusalem to present him to the Lord. (Luke 2: 22).

When Joseph and Mary had done everything required by the Law of the Lord, they returned to Galilee to their home town of Nazareth. (Luke 2: 39).

There is no suggestion here of the flight into Egypt and the wicked Herod. The two accounts cannot both be correct.

What about the Star in the East? The Bible reports that it went ahead of the Magi and stopped over the place where the child was:

After they (the Wise Men) *had heard the king* (Herod), *they went on their way, and the star they had seen in the east went ahead of them until it stopped over the place where the child was. When they saw the star, they were overjoyed. On coming to the house, they saw the child with his mother Mary, and they bowed down and worshipped him. Then they opened their treasures and presented him with gifts of gold and of incense and of myrrh."* (Matt. 2: 9 – 11).

Potentially here, we have a brilliant chance for science and Christianity to link up. If there was a bright moving star, what could it be? The most likely answer would be a comet. Halley's comet appears regularly every 79 years, and it is easy to calculate that it would have made one of its regular fly pasts in 12 BCE, but that is too early. Another possibility would be a nova, which in simple terms means an exploding star. Here we are on safer ground because there was a nova in 5 BCE, which was visible to Chinese astronomers for 70 days. So this bright nova could have been the star mentioned in Matthew's Gospel. Thus it does seem quite likely that Jesus was born about 5 BCE, but once again, this is no proof, and we are no nearer to deciding on the Virgin Birth.

So what can we deduce about the Virgin Birth? Christians believe in the Virgin Birth, and it remains an all important part of the Christian doctrine, especially in the Roman Catholic Church. The Christian argument often runs along the lines: given that Jesus was fully Divine and fully human, this can only happen if he had a human mother and God as his Divine father. And yes, it was a miracle, but this would be no problem to an all-powerful God. After all, if we accept that the Resurrection was the ultimate miracle, as we shall see in Chapter 7, then the miracle of a Virgin Birth should be no problem and perfectly in order. And yet did it really happen? Do we go along the line of the Jesus of Faith, which fully accepts the miraculous Virgin Birth and no questions asked, or, do we look at the Historical Jesus which has considerable difficulty with the whole doctrine? Many scholars to-day, such as Geza Vermes, a leading authority on Jesus, believe that the infancy stories are all pure legend or metaphorical and that they were added on to the Gospels of Matthew and Luke at a later date. Sadly, there is still a considerable schism and controversy here and it may yet be some time before the two sides are even prepared to take part in meaningful discussions on this one.

In the final analysis, and in all honesty, it is difficult to be completely sure of this. I am agnostic on this subject. Many scholars would now argue that from an historical point of view,

Jesus was born before the death of Herod the Great in 4 BCE and that Mary and Joseph were his parents. One problem here is that there were only three people who would probably have known the full facts here: that is Joseph, Mary and Jesus himself. By contrast, as we shall see in Chapter 7, there is much stronger evidence for the Resurrection, because there were dozens of people who were witnesses. But for the birth of Jesus, who else could have known the true facts? One possible solution, as a number of Protestant and Catholic theologians have argued, is why not have Joseph still being the bodily father of Jesus, while at the same time, stating that this does not have to *exclude* the fatherhood of God? This seems to me to be a very plausible and sensible way forward.

What does matter, and here both sides would agree, is that the Christmas stories in Matthew and Luke are preserved because they are a delight to all Christians and especially to children; that is apart from the one terrible story of the murder of the innocents by the dreadful Herod:

When Herod realised that he had been outwitted by the Magi, he was furious, and he gave orders to kill all the boys in Bethlehem and its vicinity who were two years and under, in accordance with the time he had learned from the Magi. (Matt. 2: 16).

This is at odds with the Christmas story; there is no shred of evidence of it happening outside Matthew's Gospel and in my view this story is best disregarded, at least when it is being told to children. However, it has to be admitted that Herod was so brutal, that he would have been quite capable of such an atrocity.

My views on the Virgin Birth may not go down too well with many people in the pews, but does it *really* matter if the stories turn out not to be historically true? If we examine the first two chapters of Matthew, they are in a radically different style to the rest of the Gospel, and thus may well have been written later by a different author. The same applies for the first two chapters of Luke. If these two chapters in both Matthew and Luke had not existed, would this really have made that big a difference to the life of Jesus? What we can say is that the Nativity stories are quite brilliant whichever way we look at them. They have been immensely popular and have lasted so well for 2,000 years. For myself, if scholars decide that these stories really are myth, it would *have no effect at all on my faith and my belief in God and Jesus.*

In summary, we can conclude the following:

1. Matthew, Luke and the non-Canonical Gospel of James record the Virgin Birth.

2. This has been part of the Christian teaching ever since.

3. There is no evidence of this anywhere else in the New Testament – i.e. in the other two Gospels and all of Paul's writings.

4. Mary had at least six other children after Jesus - no suggestion of a Virgin Birth there.

5. Therefore, she did not remain a virgin, even if she was one when Jesus was born.

6.   The historicity of the Virgin Birth remains open to question.

7.   *This should not be a deal breaker.*

Chapter 6:
Jesus 2: His Life and Death.

In this chapter, I am going to look at the life of Jesus. The Christian Faith teaches us that he was fully human and yet fully divine. I am going to select a few of the stories from the gospels that show something of the nature of Jesus with special emphasis on the human side. After his birth, the first 30 or so years of Jesus' life are known as the "Hidden Years". With just one exception, we know nothing about these years. It seems that these were years of development and the gradual realisation by Jesus of just who he was.

The one exception is the fascinating story of Jesus at the Temple when he was 12 years old as given in Luke's Gospel, Chapter 2 verses 41 – 50. The story describes how every year Mary and Joseph went up to Jerusalem for the Feast of the Passover. Afterwards, Jesus went missing, but his parents started back for Nazareth thinking that he was in the company of their relatives or friends. But he wasn't, and his parents went back to Jerusalem to look for him. Verses 46 onwards state:

After three days they found him in the temple court, sitting amongst the teachers, listening to them and asking them questions. Everyone who heard him was amazed at his understanding and his answers. When his parents saw him, they were astonished. His mother said to him, "Son, why have you treated us like this? Your father and I have been anxiously searching for you." "Why were you searching for me?" he asked. "Didn't you know that I had to be in my Father's house?" (Luke 2: 46 - 49)

At this stage in Luke's Gospel, the story breaks off:

But they did not understand what he was saying to them. (Luke 2: 50).

Interestingly, the story is exactly mirrored in the non-Canonical Infancy "Gospel" of Thomas which instead of verse 50, has this addition:

The scribes and Pharisees said, "Are you the mother of this child?" She replied, "I am." They said to her, "You are most fortunate among women, because God has blessed the fruit of your womb. For we have never seen or heard of such glory, such virtue and wisdom."

This Gospel has nothing to do with the Gospel of Thomas, mentioned in Chapter 2, but is a largely apocryphal writing professing to be a record of miracles performed by Jesus while still a child. It is probable that the author made up the stories and then ended up by copying this well-known account of Jesus from Luke's Gospel. But then the author added this extra verse, which was either made up, or if it came from a common source used by Luke, why did Luke omit the verse? Or, was the verse merely added much later by the author of Thomas' "Gospel"? Either way, it does seem that at 12 years old, Jesus was very advanced for his age, and even precocious, in the way he addresses his mother.

After that until the age of about 30, we know nothing about Jesus. As stated earlier, they are the "Hidden Years" when he gradually finds out what his mission in life is. It is true that there are various non-canonical "Gospels", in particular the Infancy "Gospel" of James and the Infancy "Gospel" of Thomas, as mentioned earlier. These "Gospels" give various stories about the boy Jesus such as the time when he and his friends made some clay sparrows. Jesus, aged just five, then clapped his hands and shouted "Fly away!" to which the clay birds became living sparrows that flew away chirping. Entertaining as this and other stories are, they were written much later in the second or third century CE and are pure myth.

For the three years beginning with the time of Jesus' Baptism in the River Jordan by John the Baptist, which is reported in all four canonical Gospels, up until the Crucifixion, there are dozens of stories in the Gospels. I am going to concentrate first on the ones that illustrate Jesus' human nature, and also a few that have an especial appeal to me.

We start with St Mark's Gospel:

Then Jesus entered a house, and again a crowd gathered, so that he and his disciples were not even able to eat. When his family heard about this, they went to take charge of him, for they said, "He is out of his mind." (Mark 3: 20 – 21).

True to form, these verses are only in Mark's Gospel and were edited out by both Matthew and Luke. It was early in his ministry but Jesus had already performed a number of healing miracles. His family thought him mad. Later in verse 32 of the same chapter, his mother and brothers came looking for him. Because these stories sound authentic, they can be seen as a source of embarrassment to the Christian Faith, and because they were edited out by both Matthew and Luke, nevertheless they seem all too likely to be true.

Then there are times when Jesus is particularly vitriolic towards his enemies, the teachers of the law and the Pharisees, who think themselves above everyone else. This is clearly stated in Matthew's Gospel when Jesus has a real go at the Pharisees with their evil ways and with good reason.

"You snakes! You brood of vipers! How will you escape being condemned to hell?" (Matt. 23: 33).

This is hardly "Gentle Jesus meek and mild"! Herod (one of the sons of the evil Herod in the nativity stories) was a particular enemy. Jesus replies to some otherwise friendly Pharisees who had come to warn him that Herod was out to kill him:

*"Go tell that **FOX** 'I will drive out demons and heal people to-day and to-morrow, and on the third day I will reach my goal.'"* (Luke 14: 32).

In addition, there is the well-known occasion when Jesus went quite wild overturning the tables of the money changers in the temple, reported in all four gospels. Another side of the "human" Jesus comes in the garden of Gethsemane when Jesus became "deeply distressed and troubled", not surprisingly given that he knew what was likely to be in store for him. A sad part of this story is that it is the one time that Jesus really did ask his disciples for some help, but they were all too exhausted and kept sleeping. These are just a few of the examples in the gospels that show the very human side of Jesus.

He was also a brilliant teacher. There is the Sermon on the Mount in Matthew's Gospel, with a shortened version in Luke's Gospel. But it is his parables that show Jesus at his best. The parables of the Sower, the Prodigal Son and the Good Samaritan are particular favourites of mine. These are down-to-earth stories about country folk that were easily understood, and that were passed on from person to person by oral tradition. In the case of the Prodigal Son, this story had been passed around for long before the time of Jesus. There is a version of it in early Hindu culture. Nevertheless, the story of the Prodigal Son is a masterpiece of storytelling. There is the point of view of the younger son, who at least had some fun for a while, the point of view of the most compassionate father and, finally, the point of view of the smug elder son, (Luke Chapter 15, verses 11 – 32). There is a huge amount of teaching in this very human story. This is a good example of a story in the Bible that is not historically true, but nevertheless has a huge amount of truth in the meaning. Incidentally, the story of Jonah being swallowed by a whale in the Old Testament should also be taken as a parable even though it is not portrayed as such. Finally, as I mentioned in Chapter 2, there are only two parables in John's Gospel, the Good Shepherd (John 10: 1 – 18) and the True Vine (John 15: 1 – 8).

All the stories quoted so far can be found in the Synoptic Gospels. But there is one story only found in John's Gospel that brings out another side of Jesus' nature. This is the story of the conversation that Jesus had with a Samaritan woman at Jacob's Well, which is in John Chapter 4. Jesus was tired after a long journey and sat down by the well for a rest. Presently a Samaritan woman came to draw water and Jesus asked her for a drink of water. She was an intelligent woman and they indulge in quite a long conversation about the spring of water and eternal life.

The Samaritan woman said to him, "You are a Jew and I am a Samaritan woman. How can you ask me for a drink?" (For Jews do not associate with Samaritans). Jesus answered her, "If you knew the gift of God and who it is that asks you for a drink, you would have asked him and he would have given you living water." "Sir," the woman said, "you have nothing to draw with and the well is deep. Where can you get this living water? Are you greater than our father Jacob, who gave us the well and drank from it himself, as did also his sons and his flocks and herds?" Jesus answered, "Everyone who drinks this water will be thirsty again, but whoever drinks the water I give him will never thirst. Indeed the water I give him will become in him a spring of water welling up to eternal life." The woman said to him, "Sir, give me this water so that I won't get thirsty and have to keep coming here to draw water." He told her, "Go, call your husband and come back." "I have no husband," she replied. Jesus said to her, "You are right when you say you have no husband. The fact is, you have had five husbands, and the man you now have is not your husband. What you have said is quite true." "Sir", the woman said, "I can see that you are a prophet". (John 4: 9 – 19)

Wow! Some woman! I imagine this woman as an attractive 30-something who has had no problem in having any man she wanted. We are not told what has happened to the five husbands, whether she has dispensed with them, whether they have just cleared off because they couldn't stand the pace, or perhaps most likely, they have simply just died. And true to modern form, for her latest man, she has given up on the idea of marriage and is just living with him. Anyway, she meets up with Jesus and is immediately struck by someone with a tremendous charisma. Here was a MAN who really attracted her, so she plays her cards as best as she knows how. I do not doubt that when she says, "*I have no husband,*" she is fluttering her eyelids. But it is Jesus who wins this *repartée* with his kindly but much amused reply. Apart from being a delightful story, what does this show us? It shows to me that Jesus did have a sense of humour, and also, that he did have this tremendous charisma, which this woman of the world saw immediately. It also shows that Jesus was quite happy to break with convention and speak to this woman who was a stranger. The Samaritan woman then went on to tell her friends how she had found Jesus the Messiah, and thus she became the first female spreader of the gospel.

There are other women in the gospels who clearly adored Jesus: Mary Magdalene was one, and I shall mention her in the next chapter. There was also the incident when Jesus visited the home of the sisters Martha and Mary. The younger sister Mary spent her time during a visit of Jesus, sitting at his feet just listening to him, while poor Martha fussed around doing all the work. All she got for that was a ticking off from Jesus!

She had a sister called Mary, who sat at the Lord's feet listening to what he said. But Martha was distracted by all the preparations that had to be made. She came to him and asked, "Lord, don't you care that my sister has left me to do the work by myself? Tell her to help me!" "Martha, Martha," the Lord answered, "you are worried and upset by many things, but only one thing is needed. Mary has chosen what is better, and it will not be taken away from her." (Luke 10: 39 – 42).

It is noteworthy that many of these stories concern women. Jesus had a number of women friends and they seem to play a far bigger role in his life than women appear to have done in the lives of leaders of other great faiths and cultures. However, at no stage was there any suggestion that Jesus was romantically involved with any of them; they were just very good friends.

These are just a brief selection of a few stories from the gospels, designed to show that Jesus had a very human side. There are, of course, many other stories that could have been selected. But in summary, we can conclude that Jesus was not meek and mild, but rather he had an iron character and could be angry and impatient. He was also highly intelligent and extremely gifted in debate. He had a wonderful habit of being able to throw a question back to his questioners in a way that they could not answer. But he loved small children and felt pity for the underdog. He also had a number of female friends, who clearly cared for him very much.

We turn now to the more divine side of Jesus. There are the stories of the Baptism of Jesus by John the Baptist, and the Transfiguration which come in all three synoptic gospels. However it is the miracles of Jesus that hold particular interest in showing us his divine nature.

Broadly speaking the miracles divide into three distinct types. First, there are the six exorcisms, of which the Gerasene (or Gadarene) Demon (Mark 5: 1 – 20, Matthew 8: 28 – 34 and Luke 8: 26 – 39) and the Boy with the Epileptic Spirit (Mark 9: 14 – 29, Matthew (17: 14 – 20, Luke 9: 37 - 43) are perhaps the best known examples. In the case of the Gerasene Demon, it really does seem that the man was possessed by some evil spirit or spirits from the next world. Anyway, Jesus had the power to command the spirit to move on, which it did into the Gerasene swine.

The boy with the epileptic spirit may likewise have been possessed by a really horrible spirit as was believed to be the case at the time, or he may have just had bad epilepsy, as told in Mark Chapter 9. Jesus together with Peter, James and John (the first "division" of the disciples), had been away up a high mountain (we are not told the name of the mountain) for the Transfiguration, when the remaining disciples had tried to heal the boy who was foaming at the mouth and being thrown to the ground, having what appears to have been epileptic fits. But they failed and when Jesus returned, the boy's family asked for healing from Jesus for the boy, the father saying that he was a true believer.

When Jesus saw that a crowd was running to the scene, he rebuked the evil spirit. "You deaf and mute spirit," he said, I

*command you, come out of him and never enter him again."
The spirit shrieked, convulsed him violently and came out. The
boy looked so much like a corpse that many said, "He's dead."
But Jesus took him by the hand and lifted him to his feet, and
he stood up. After Jesus had gone indoors, his disciples asked
him privately, "Why couldn't we drive him out?" He replied,
"This kind can come out only by prayer."* (Mark 9: 25 – 29).

Notice that this is really a two stage process, and I shall return
to this theme in the next section on healing. It is only in Mark
that the two stage process is described. In the other two
synoptic gospels, the healing is instant. It also sounds very
dramatic with the boy lying perfectly still as if dead, according
to Mark and I can well imagine the indignation of the crowd
starting to rise at this point. To me it sounds like a vivid
description of an all too true incident. It also seems that both a
certain amount of "know-how" and faith are needed.

A third interesting exorcism concerns the faith of a Syro-
Phoenician woman who had a daughter with a demon.

*Jesus left that place and went to the vicinity of Tyre. He entered
a house and did not want anyone to know it; yet he could not
keep his presence secret. In fact, as soon as she heard about
him, a woman whose little daughter was possessed by an evil
spirit came and fell at his feet. The woman was a Greek, born
in Syrian Phoenicia. She begged Jesus to drive the demon out
of her daughter. "First let the children eat all they want," he
told her, for it is not right to take the children's bread and toss
it to their dogs." "Yes, Lord," she replied, "but even the dogs
under the table eat the children's crumbs." Then he told her,
"For such a reply, you may go; the demon has left your*

daughter." She went home and found her child lying on the bed, and the demon gone. (Mark 7: 24 – 30).

There is a similar account of the Syro-Phoenician woman in Matthew's Gospel, Chapter 15, verses 21 – 28. It seems that at first Jesus was reluctant to be bothered with this woman because she was a foreigner, an interesting contrast to his ready conversation with the Samaritan woman. Generally, Jesus was not keen just to satisfy people's desire for a dramatic miracle, but then on the other hand he was often filled with compassion for those who pleaded with him for a cure. In the case of the Syro-Phoenician woman, she persisted in the way that any mother would with a sick child. Jesus was so impressed by her faith that he relented, and the healing took place. To me, this story is indicative of the process of Jesus gradually coming to realise that he was not on Earth just for the people of Israel, that is the Jews, but for everyone.

At the time of Jesus, the casting out of demons was very much part of the culture of the day. It is not part of our culture to-day, and anyone so afflicted would probably be recommended to see a psychiatrist. And yet, given my experience with a certain poltergeist, as described in Chapter 3, mischievous or even evil spirits do exist in the next world. On rare occasions it does seem possible that such an entity might invade a vulnerable person. Jesus would have known about this and also how to deal with these spirits. To-day, the Church of England and the Roman Catholic Church do have a service for exorcism, but it is sparingly used.

The second type of miracle is the healings and raisings from the dead. There are about 19 healing miracles spread throughout the four gospels. There are two healing miracles that can hold our attention for the moment. The first is the healing of the blind man at Bethsaida as reported in Mark's Gospel. The crowd brought a blind man to Jesus for healing:

He took the blind man by the hand and led him outside the village. When he had spat on the man's eyes and put his hands on him, Jesus asked, "Do you see anything?" He looked up and said, "I see people; they look like trees walking around." Once more Jesus put his hands on the man's eyes. Then his eyes were opened, his sight was restored, and he saw everything clearly, Jesus sent him home saying, "Don't go into the village." (Mark 8: 23 – 25).

This is one of the few stories that is unique to Mark. The healing was not instantaneous, and therefore has a real ring of truth about it. Matthew and Luke omit the story – perhaps they found it a little awkward, the fact that the healing was not instantaneous. We should compare this with the Boy with the Epileptic Spirit, described earlier. There was nothing too unusual about this. There were a number of other charismatic prophets around at this time who were supposed to have performed healing miracles. Some 900 years earlier, the two O.T. books of Kings record Elijah and Elisha performing healing miracles on a limited scale. But Jesus was clearly much more powerful than any of them.

The second healing miracle was the raising of Lazarus from the dead, and this was a "Big One". This was not just a healing but a raising from the dead. In some ways this could be seen as a forerunner of the Resurrection. In this case Lazarus had been dead for four days and was thus well beyond the Point Of No

Return. This is a lot more powerful than just a healing. His two sisters, Martha and Mary, whom we have already come across in this chapter, were in great distress about the loss of their beloved brother. This miracle is only recorded in John's Gospel, Chapter 11:

When Mary reached the place where Jesus was and saw him, she fell at his feet and said, "Lord, if you had been here, my brother would not have died." When Jesus saw her weeping, and the Jews who had come along with her also weeping, he was deeply moved in spirit and troubled. "Where have you laid him?" he asked. "Come and see, Lord," they replied. Jesus wept. (These two words form the shortest verse in the bible). *Then the Jews said, "See how he loved him!" But some of them said, "Could not he who opened the eyes of the blind man have kept this man from dying?" Jesus, once more deeply moved, came to the tomb. It was a cave with a stone laid across the entrance. "Take away the stone," he said. "But, Lord," said Martha, the sister of the dead man, "by this time there is a bad odour, for he has been there four days."* (This is the ever-practical Martha in full flow, but it does add a ring of truth to the story). *Then Jesus said, "Did I not tell you that if you believed, you would see the glory of God?" So they took away the stone. Then Jesus looked up and said, "Father I thank you that you have heard me. I knew that you always hear me, but I said this for the benefit of the people standing here, that they may believe that you sent me." When he had said this, Jesus called in a loud voice, "Lazarus, come out!" The dead man came out, his hands and feet wrapped with strips of linen, and a cloth around his face. Jesus said to them, "Take off the grave clothes and let him go."* (John 11: 32 – 44).

This is a difficult one. Why was such a spectacular miracle not recorded in any of the Synoptics? Did it really happen as reported in John's Gospel? Or was it a story made up by the writers of John's Gospel, written some 60 or so years later as once again being something that Jesus might have done? I am agnostic on this one. All I can suggest is that because the miracle was only recorded in John's Gospel, at least some degree of exaggeration may have crept in. But it may be that the miracle was exactly as recorded, in which case, similar to the Resurrection, this really was astounding. Incidentally, this story, if true, also shows the very human side to Jesus because he appears to be genuinely upset. I shall deal further with the subject of Healing *per se* in Chapter 11 in a separate section. For the moment, we can see that Jesus healed many people, as mentioned early on in Mark's Gospel:

That evening after sunset the people brought to Jesus all the sick and demon-possessed. The whole town gathered at the door, and Jesus healed many who had various diseases. He also drove out many demons, but he would not let the demons speak because they knew who he was. (Mark 1: 32 – 34).

The important point to realise is that people *firmly believed that Jesus was a great healer*. The evidence for this is overwhelming. And yet, it appears that even Jesus did not have unlimited powers of healing. There was a time when Jesus had returned to his home town, presumably Nazareth:

Jesus said to them, "Only in his home town, among his relatives and in his own house is a prophet without honour." He could not do any miracles there, except lay his hands on a few sick people and heal them. And he was amazed at their lack of faith. (Mark 6: 4 – 6).

The third type of miracle could be called the nature wonders, or the miracles against the laws of nature. There are seven of them. The most well-known examples include turning water into wine, the stilling of the storm on the Sea of Galilee, the walking on the water and the feedings of the four and five thousand. The first miracle as recorded by John was the turning of water into wine at the wedding feast at Cana in Galilee. As this was again only recorded in John's Gospel, written so much later, one cannot help wondering whether this was originally some kind of parable that got embroidered with its continual retelling. In any case, filling six stone water jars each holding some twenty to thirty gallons means at least 120 gallons of wine, enough for a drunken orgy for even the largest wedding feast!

There has been speculation that when Jesus walked on the Sea of Galilee he was using some law of physics, known well enough to him, but unknown to us, but this sounds hardly credible. If this sort of miracle happened as reported in Matthew, Mark and John, then it seems simplest to accept it at face value as a real miracle, and leave it at that.

It is reasonable to ask, "Did these miracles happen as reported in the gospels?" "Are they historically true?" As there is no way of confirming the truth behind the miracles, in my experience, most historians remain pretty sceptical on this subject. To the Christian they are a matter of belief. However, there is one thing that the historian can be sure about and that is during Jesus' life and for a long time afterwards, there grew up a very strong belief and indeed certainty amongst various groups that Jesus really did perform miracles.

Parts of John's Gospel are quite difficult, and in many ways it is very different from the three Synoptic Gospels. This especially applies to the four Chapters 14 - 17, when Jesus gives a long and often puzzling discourse on this world and the next world. I have already mentioned John, Chapter 14, verse 2 about *"In my father's house there are many rooms"*, in Chapter 3 of this book. This is followed by:

*Thomas said to him, "Lord, we do not know where you are going, so how can we know the way?" Jesus answered, "I am the way and the truth and the life. **No-one comes to the Father except through me."*** (John 14: 5 – 6).

This is a difficult one. There are many Christians of a more fundalmentalist inclination who accept this at face value, and then conclude that Judaism, Islam, Buddhism, Hinduism and all other religions are of no value. In my view this is no way to any sort of rapprochement with believers from other religions, as I intend to show in Chapter 9. One way through this moral maze would be to realize that the author of John's Gospel was writing some 60 years later, as mentioned earlier in this chapter. These famous words may have been put into Jesus' mouth because the author thought that this is what Jesus would have said. Another approach is to consider that while this is absolutely right for Christians, there are other ways up the mountain, perhaps by a very different route, but the end result remains God or Allah or Whoever, and a life after this one at the top of the mountain. A curious saying of Jesus comes in another part of John's Gospel when he is talking about the Good Shepherd and his Flock:

"I have other sheep that are not of this sheep pen. I must bring them also. They too will listen to my voice, and there will be one flock and one shepherd." (John 10: 16).

It is not clear whether he is referring to the Gentiles or even to people of other religions, but it does seem that in Jesus' eyes the Jews were not the only ones who were around.

There are, of course, very many other wonderful events that happened during Jesus' life that show both his human and divine nature. All I have shown here is a selection of happenings that bring out both his natures. We come, finally, on to the Passiontide including the Crucifixion and the death of Jesus on Good Friday. The Passiontide is traditionally the final two weeks of Lent depicting the last few days of Jesus' life on earth. These events are recorded in considerable detail in all four Gospels. Although there are some differences in detail, the Gospels are in broad agreement as to what happened. Jesus has his triumphal entry into Jerusalem riding on a donkey, but this is soon followed by the Last Supper, his agony, betrayal and arrest in the Garden of Gethsemane, followed by his trial. The historian would have no trouble with these events, which must have been very much as reported in the Gospels. The Last Supper was timed to coincide with the Jewish Passover, which is the spring festival each year commemorating the deliverance of the Israelites from being held captive in Egypt. One big discrepancy, however, is that John's Gospel has Jesus crucified on the afternoon before the Passover Supper, and so there is no Last Supper as in the three synoptic Gospels. There can be no doubt at all, even to unbelievers, that Jesus was crucified. Although the utterances of Jesus upon the cross vary, the event is clearly reported in considerable detail in all four Gospels, and also in the writings of Josephus. Crucifixion was a common enough occurrence at this time and was the way the Romans kept discipline throughout their empire. Jesus was put to death because he was an agitator and popular with the masses including the poor and downcast. He upset all those in authority including the fussy Pharisees. It was a particularly cruel, sadistic and painful form of death, and, important as it is, I do not wish to dwell upon this topic. It is true that the occasional tough individual hung on the cross for up to three days before expiring, but Jesus died relatively quickly in about three hours on the same day that he was crucified. After all that he had been through, he must have been physically exhausted. What happened two days later or "on the third day" is far more important and quite amazing, as we shall see in the next chapter.

Chapter 7:
Jesus 3: The
Resurrection.

This is the really "BIG ONE". Christianity teaches us that Jesus Christ rose from the dead on the first Easter Sunday, and upon this quite amazing event, the whole belief system depends. Quite simply: *If there was no Resurrection, there would be no Christianity:*

And if Christ had not been raised, our preaching is useless and so is your faith. (1 Corinthians 15: 14).

So wrote St Paul to the Corinthians. Something very dramatic happened on that first Easter morning. So, *what really took place?* Well, we will look at the accounts in all four Gospels and in the remainder of the New Testament. Between the four Gospels, there are the usual sharp variations.

We begin with the Empty Tomb. Early on that Sunday morning certain women hurried to the tomb with spices in order to anoint the body, but they were rather fussed because they knew a huge stone or boulder would be blocking the entrance to the tomb where they believed Jesus' body lay. Imagine their intense alarm when they arrived at the tomb to find that the stone had been rolled away and Jesus' body had vanished! Immediately we come to the differences between the Gospels, with variation as to who the women were:

Mark: Mary Magdalene, Mary the mother of James, Salome.

Matthew: Mary Magdalene, "the other Mary", (the mother of James?).

Luke: Mary Magdalene, Joanna, Mary the mother of James.

John: Mary Magdalene.

Thus we can take it that one, two or three women arrived at the tomb, one of whom was Mary Magdalene. The important point here is that the story is very likely to be true because if the story were a legend, women would not have been chosen to discover the Empty Tomb.   As stated in Chapter 2, at the time women were considered to be very much second-class citizens and any evidence they gave in court was considered to be totally unreliable.   Thus we can be reasonably certain that the Empty Tomb was indeed discovered by Mary Magdalene and possibly other women. However, it is important to realise that just because the tomb was empty of Jesus' body, this does not in itself mean that he had risen from the dead. We shall return to the Empty Tomb and Mary Magdalene later in this chapter.

What the women discovered inside the tomb can give us a fair description of how the four Evangelists treated the scene. In each Gospel, one or two young men are discovered sitting in the tomb:

Mark: A young man dressed in a white robe sitting on the right side.

Matthew: A young man whose appearance was like lightning and whose clothes were white as snow.

Luke: Two men in clothes that gleamed like lightning.

John: Two angels in white seated at where Jesus' body had been.

As usual, it is the Mark version that is the most plausible. We have here a good example of how a story can be embellished with frequent telling. Matthew in particular really does seem to have gone over the top. Also, the fact that these reports are inconsistent, in a curious way, adds to their authenticity. After something dramatic happens, such as a road accident, the various witnesses in their excitement and anxiety, tend to report the incident but with different details. This may well have been the case with the Empty Tomb. Imagine the women's amazement and fear.

However, it is the appearances of the risen Jesus on that day, and the days following that are crucial. Very unfortunately, Mark's Gospel breaks off at this stage:

Trembling and bewildered, the women went out and fled from the tomb. They said nothing to anyone, because they were afraid..... (Mark 16: 8)

I do not wonder that they were terrified by the scene. Sadly, however, it seems that the last part of the gospel has gone missing. The earliest manuscripts end abruptly at this stage, probably in mid-sentence. It seems likely that the last page of the original parchment got torn off presumably by accident, as I mentioned in Chapter 2. Some Bibles include verses 9 – 20 printed but these were probably added a century or more later and appear not to be the work and style of the writer of Mark's

Gospel. These verses merely give a brief summary of what comes in the other gospels and are thus do not appear to be authentic. In any case they appear rather bland and not in the all action style of most of Mark's Gospel. If ever the original ending of the Gospel is discovered, it would be a sensation!

Matthew's Gospel describes two short appearances of Jesus, without any worthwhile detail. Jesus appears briefly to his disciples and instructs them to proceed to Galilee where he will see them again. Finally he appears to his disciples on an unnamed mountain in Galilee. This does not tell us very much but at least the Gospel ends on a high: After a few brief instructions from Jesus, he says:

"And surely I am with you always, to the very end of the age." (Matt. 28: 20).

However, it is the Gospels of Luke and John that tell us a great deal more. In Luke, Chapter 24, verses 13 – 29, we have the well-known scene on the road to Emmaus, sometime later on the day of the Resurrection. Two of the disciples were walking along the road to Emmaus which is about 7 miles from Jerusalem. One of them was called Cleopas, who may have been a brother of Joseph. The two of them were deep in conversation about the strange events of that morning when they were joined by a stranger, who enquired what they were discussing. The two disciples were amazed to find that the stranger was friendly enough, but appeared to know nothing of what had happened:

One of them, named Cleopas, asked him (the stranger), *"Are you only a visitor to Jerusalem and do not know these things that have happened there in these days?" "What things?" he asked. "About Jesus of Nazareth," they replied. "He was a prophet, powerful in word and deed before God and all the people."* (Luke: 24: 18 – 19).

The disciples then go on and describe the Crucifixion and apparent Resurrection. The stranger was indeed Jesus, but for some reason, *they did not recognise him.* Eventually, when they reached their destination in Emmaus, Jesus wanted to go on further but it was late in the day and they urged him to stay with them.

When he (Jesus) *was at the table with them, he took bread, gave thanks, broke it and began to give it to them. Then their eyes were opened and they recognised him, and he disappeared from their sight.* (Luke 24: 30 – 31).

This sounds really weird. Jesus has the ability to appear and vanish at will and also to be unrecognisable. But there is more to it than this. Verse 36 of the same chapter goes on to describe how an unknown number of disciples were subsequently gathered together when Jesus suddenly appeared and stood amongst them, saying, *"Peace be with you."* They were then startled and frightened out of their wits and no wonder. They thought that what they were seeing was a ghost:

He (Jesus) *said to them, "Why are you troubled, and why do doubts arise in your minds? Look at my hands and feet. It is I myself! Touch me and see; a ghost does not have flesh and bones, as you see I have." When he had said this, he showed them his hands and feet. And while they still did not believe it because of joy and amazement, he asked them, "Do you have anything here to eat?" They gave him a piece of broiled fish, and he took it and ate it in their presence.* (Luke 24: 38 – 42).

No ghost that I have ever heard about has a healthy appetite! Furthermore, his flesh and bones appear to be real and able to be touched.

John's Gospel also describes some quite different appearances of Jesus after the Resurrection. In Chapter 20, Jesus appears to his disciples, but for some reason Thomas was absent. They then described the scene to Thomas, but poor Thomas, he had "doubts", so he has been known as "Doubting Thomas" ever since. But Jesus subsequently appeared to all the disciples including Thomas who then believed and all was well. Jesus encouraged Thomas to put his finger at the point of Jesus' body where particular wounds were. So it would seem that Jesus still bore the marks of his Crucifixion. Chapter 21 describes the scene sometime later by the Sea of Galilee when some of the disciples go fishing and Jesus again appears. This final chapter of John's Gospel comes as something of an epilogue which was probably added later and is in a quite different style. Most scholars to-day think that the chapter was written by a different author, possibly a disciple of John, and thus sounds less authentic.

However, it is the first appearance of Jesus immediately after the Resurrection when he appeared to Mary Magdalene in John's Gospel that holds a particular interest for me. A word first about Mary Magdalene: she appears briefly a few times in the Gospels, but we really know very little about her. We first come across her in Luke, Chapter 8, verses 2 and 3 when Jesus relieved her of seven devils or demons, after which she followed him. She was a woman of good character who had experienced Jesus' healing powers. Furthermore she was clearly a loving friend of Jesus and the disciples, often helping to look after them. She was present at the Crucifixion and then at the Resurrection. The belief that she was originally a prostitute rests merely on tradition, because she has been confused wrongly with the woman who had lead a "sinful life", and who had spent some time kissing Jesus' feet and pouring perfume on them, as described in Luke, Chapter 7, verses 36 - 50. Poor Mary Magdalene has suffered from a very undeservedly poor press over the centuries. The damage was done when in the year 591 CE Pope Gregory the Great declared that Mary Magdalene was a whore. This was quietly retracted by the Vatican in 1969 as being completely wrong. The trouble has been that there have been so many paintings of a nude or semi-nude lady purporting to be Mary Magdalene. This gave a chance for a degree of erotica under the disguise of religion. But the damage was done and she is portrayed in many films as a prostitute. Nor is there any historical evidence that after the Resurrection Mary Magdalene cleared off with Jesus, married him and had a family by him. These stories are pure legend and a complete distraction, even though they are portrayed in the book "*The Da Vinci Code*" by Dan Brown as fact. Nevertheless, it would be reasonable to assume that, being close to Jesus, she was in love with him – and why not?

This is the amazing scene as described in John's Gospel:

Then the disciples went back to their homes, but Mary stood outside the tomb crying. As she wept, she bent over to look into the tomb and saw two angels in white, seated where Jesus' body had been, one at the head and the other at the foot. They asked her, "Woman, why are you crying?" "They have taken my Lord away," she said, "and I don't know where they have put him." At this she turned round and saw Jesus standing there, but she did not realise that it was Jesus. "Woman," he said, "why are you crying? Who is it you are looking for?" **Thinking he was the gardener,** *she said, "Sir, if you have carried him away, tell me where you have put him, and I will get him." Jesus said to her, "Mary." She turned towards him and cried out in Aramaic, "Rabboni!" (which means Teacher). Jesus said,* **"Do not hold on to me, for I have not yet returned to the Father.** *Go instead to my brothers and tell them, 'I am returning to my Father and your Father, to my God and your God.'" Mary Magdalene went to the disciples with the news: "I have seen the Lord!" And she told them that he had said these things to her.* (John 20: 10 – 18).

Mary is distraught because she thinks someone has stolen the body of Jesus and cleared off. She sees a man standing nearby whom *she takes to be the gardener.* Surely she would have recognised Jesus, *but she does not.* This was further evidence that Jesus had changed in appearance. Mary did not at first recognise Jesus, in the same way that the disciples on the road to Emmaus did not recognise Jesus. It was not until he said her name, "Mary" that she immediately recognised his voice and realised who this figure was. And how does she react? She is so overjoyed that she immediately moves towards him wanting to embrace him – all very natural.

This now leads on to the famous scene that has been painted many times by various artists known as the *"Noli me tangere"* or "Do not touch me".   For some strange reason Jesus had not yet "returned to the Father", whatever that may mean, and could not be touched. There seemed no problem about this later on when the disciples, including Doubting Thomas, came along.   What this implies remains a complete mystery. But it does have the ring of truth about it.

Finally we have the Ascension:

When he (Jesus) *had led them* (the disciples) *out to the vicinity of Bethany, he lifted up his hands and blessed them. While he was blessing them, he left them and was taken up into heaven.* (Luke 24: 50 – 51).

It appears that Jesus just took off up into heaven and vanished. This does indeed sound rather fanciful.   The evidence for this is decidedly thin: in Matthew's Gospel and John's Gospel, there is no mention of this Ascension.   It's true that Mark's Gospel does state in Chapter 16:

After the Lord Jesus had spoken to them, he was taken up into heaven and he sat at the right hand of God.   (Mark 16: 19).

But we saw in Chapter 2, the final 12 verses of Mark were almost certainly added on sometime later and do not sound authentic.   So it is really only in Luke's Gospel, that we have a description of what was taken to be the Ascension, and the author follows that up in Luke Volume II, that is the book of Acts, where he states:

After he (Jesus) *said this, he was taken up before their very eyes, and a cloud hid him from their sight.*   (Acts 1: 9).

This says much the same thing as in Luke. All I can suggest is that this was a figurative way of describing that Jesus, having thoroughly encouraged his disciples, just vanished and was not seen again. In this day and age, we might say something like "She's on top of the world". We do not literally mean that, but this is a figurative way of describing a girl's feelings. Well, perhaps that is how the disciples came to describe Jesus' final appearance to them.

Then nothing further happened until the time of the Pentecost, which, each year, is the Jewish Harvest Festival, 50 days after the Passover, and some 10 days after the Ascension.

So now let us return to the Resurrection and examine it carefully. As I stated at the start of this chapter, this one is really crucial. I once asked a clergyman friend of mine, "What really happened?" He paused for a moment and was about to give me some sort of standard answer that might be given from the pulpit, when he checked himself and then came out with what I thought was a very wise statement: "Peter, you will never know, but there is one thing that you can be sure of: something very dramatic happened at the time of Pentecost." He was right. We cannot be sure of exactly what happened at the time of the actual Resurrection and this event in history is not recorded in any of the four canonical Gospels. (It is true, however, that the non-canonical Gospel of Peter does give a rather crude description of three men emerging from the tomb, two of them supporting the third. The supporters are two very tall angels whose heads reached up to heaven. Written about the third century CE this was surely a rather rough and fanciful attempt to fill a gap, and therefore a myth that we can quickly dismiss).

We can and should at least examine the very dramatic *effects* that the Resurrection had on many of Jesus' closest followers. If we move on to the Acts of the Apostles, at the beginning of Chapter 2, we have:

When the day of Pentecost came, they (the disciples) *were all together in one place. Suddenly a sound like the blowing of a violent wind came from heaven and filled the whole house where they were sitting. They saw what seemed to be tongues of fire that separated and came to rest on each of them. All of them were filled with the Holy Spirit and began to speak in other tongues as the Spirit enabled them.* (Acts 2: 1 – 4).

As stated above, this happened some seven weeks after the first Easter Day, which was two days after the Jewish Passover. During those seven weeks, the disciples remained hidden and terrified of what might happen. Suddenly they were catapulted into action and found that they could speak in public and even perform miracles of healing. Some of the bystanders thought that they had had too much to drink, but they were not drunk at all, only full of the Holy Spirit. Peter became their natural leader and they had the power to go on and perform mighty words and deeds. They really felt Jesus close to them and this has all the marks of authenticity. Thus whatever really happened at the Resurrection, the disciples *firmly believed that Jesus rose from the dead and this has been the Christian belief ever since.* In fact news of Jesus' Resurrection spread like wild fire in the following months. The book of Acts gives a reliable account of the work of the disciples, led by Peter in the first half. Then in the second half, we have the travels of Paul all proclaiming the Good News of the Resurrection far and wide, even as far as Rome.

Paul's first Epistle to the Corinthians is especially relevant at this point. Paul is writing:

For what I received I passed on to you as of first importance: that Christ died for our sins according to the Scriptures, that he was buried, that he was raised on the third day according to the Scriptures, and that he appeared to Peter, and then he appeared to the Twelve. After that, he appeared to more than five hundred of the brothers at the same time, most of whom are still living, though some have fallen asleep. Then he appeared to James, then to all the apostles, and last of all he appeared to me also, as to one abnormally born. (I Corinthians 15: 3 – 8).

This is one of the earliest books in the New Testament, written about 54 or 55 CE, which is at least 10 years before the earliest of the Gospels, Mark. This letter was written to a church in the Greek city of Corinth which Paul had already visited – see Acts 18: 1 – 21. The point here is that the belief that Jesus had risen from the dead was well known and widespread, and this was long before the Gospels were written. Paul's account here is the first record of the Resurrection anywhere within the New Testament. He recorded various appearances of Jesus, some of which are not recorded in the Gospels. I particularly like the short sentence in verse 7: *Then he appeared to James.* This is the James, Jesus' brother, who is only mentioned very occasionally in the New Testament. James was not close to Paul, but at least Paul mentions the appearance. Finally, the reference that Jesus *appeared to me also*, refers to Paul's conversion as portrayed in Acts Chapter 9. Thus, although Paul had never met Jesus before the Crucifixion, he became utterly convinced of the truth of the Resurrection.

Some people have tried to argue that the Resurrection never happened because Jesus survived the Cross, and was taken down in a badly wounded condition but alive. This is the so-called "Swoon Theory". This does not add up because in all of the appearances, there is no suggestion of a badly wounded man. Over time there have been other theories such as the disciples visiting the wrong tomb or that they stole the body and hid it. These ideas also do not add up. At this time the disciples were frightened, disillusioned men who hid behind locked doors. When they did see Jesus they were slow to understand what was happening. But they did start to understand and there are several accounts of the Risen Jesus in all the Gospels, the Acts of the Apostles and some of the Epistles. Unlike the Virgin Birth stories, there is a huge amount of evidence for the Risen Jesus. Furthermore, if the disciples had invented the story, *many of them would not have been prepared to die for believing in it. No, Jesus really did die on the Cross and he really did rise up on that first Easter Sunday.* This was not as a ghost nor as the resuscitation of a dead body, but in some form and some dimension which we simply do not, as yet, understand. By all the known laws of nature, this was indeed a miracle. It seems that Jesus was now in a solid enough body, but one that may have been sufficiently different as to be unrecognisable at first. Some people, including myself, believe that once we die, we exist on "the other side" in a spiritual or so-called "Astral" body, which is similar to our human body, but nevertheless different and separate. Thus Jesus would have the power to come and visit his disciples using his Astral body.

I realise that this still leaves a lot of questions unanswered. The Gospels cannot give us concrete historical proof of the Resurrection, but we can say that they give a *reasonable explanation* of what took place. One day, when we are considerably more advanced in these matters, we may come to understand this amazing event in history better, but for the time being, we can say that this is an example of the Jesus of Mystery, that was referred to in Chapter 5.

In Summary, we can conclude the following:

1. Jesus dies upon the cross on the first Good Friday.

2. On the first Easter Sunday, certain female friends find Jesus' tomb empty.

3. These women are startled and afraid.

4. Jesus appears to Mary Magdalene and various disciples.

5. JESUS HAS RISEN FROM THE DEAD!

6. The Ascension: Jesus ascends to Heaven 40 days after the first Easter morning.

Chapter 8:
The 12 Disciples and Paul.

In this chapter, we are going to examine briefly the role of the 12 disciples and St Paul and see how they were responsible for spreading the Good News about Jesus after the Resurrection. A disciple literally means one who learns or is a pupil and anyone can have disciples. However the 12 personal followers of Jesus are generally referred to as "The Disciples". But they can also be referred to as the 12 apostles. An apostle generally means literally "anyone who is sent" out to preach the Christian Gospel and this would certainly include St Paul.

We begin with the 12 disciples, who are the men that Jesus chose to be with him and be his closest followers. They were a motley crew from the Galilee area, not particularly well educated and often slow to understand what on earth was going on with Jesus. What were their names and who were they? There are three occasions in the N.T. when there is a list of them: that is Mark Chapter 3, verses 16 – 19, Luke Chapter 6, verses 14 – 16 and Acts Chapter 1, verse 13. The first three disciples are named Simon Peter, James and his brother John. These are the "inner circle" and are the three disciples who were closest to Jesus, and also the ones whom we know most about. The remaining nine are named Andrew, Philip, Bartholomew, (or Nathanael), Matthew, Thomas, James, the son of Alphaeus, Thaddaeus, Simon the Zealot and Judas Iscariot. Apart from the final name, Judas Iscariot, the disciple who betrayed Jesus, we know little about these remaining disciples although most of them have hospitals or churches named after them, in various parts of the Christian world. What follows will be a short account of all of them.

We begin with **Peter**, or **Simon Peter** as he is sometimes known, who was the natural leader of the disciples especially after Jesus' Resurrection. We know a lot about Peter from the Gospel accounts. I always imagine him as quite a big warm hearted man, but someone who was liable to be impetuous, miss the point of what Jesus was saying and then say the wrong thing at the wrong time. In all the lists of the disciples, Peter is always the one to head the list, and in time he became the natural leader. In Chapter 6, I referred to Jesus walking on the Sea of Galilee, this being one of the seven 'nature' miracles. Matthew Chapter 14 gives a classic example of Peter's impetuous nature. Jesus is seen walking on the water of the Sea of Galilee approaching the boat much to the amazement of the disciples in their boat:

During the fourth watch of the night Jesus went out to them, walking on the lake. When the disciples saw him walking on the lake, they were terrified. "It's a ghost" they said, and cried out in fear. But Jesus immediately said to them: "Take courage! It is I. Don't be afraid." "Lord, if it's you," Peter replied, "tell me to come to you on the water." "Come," he said. Then Peter got down out of the boat and came towards Jesus. But when he saw the wind, he was afraid, and, beginning to sink, cried out, Lord, save me!" Immediately Jesus stretched out his hand and caught him. "You of little faith," he said, "why do you doubt?" (Matt. 14: 25 – 30).

Poor Peter! But this was typical of him. At least he was prepared to try and walk on the water, unlike all the other disciples. And to begin with, all went well – he did manage a few strides on the water but then disaster began to strike as soon as he saw the wind. Happily he was saved by Jesus and all was well. Then there is the story of the Transfiguration as given in the three Synoptic Gospels. The inner circle of Peter, James and John are present, and they become so flabbergasted and afraid at what they were witnessing with the appearance of Jesus, Elijah and Moses, with Jesus appearing with his dazzling white clothes. Peter feels he had better say something:

Peter said to Jesus, "Rabbi, it is good for us to be here. Let us put up three shelters – one for you, one for Moses and one for Elijah." He did not know what to say, they were so frightened. (Mark 9: 5 – 6).

Peter just said the first thing that came into his head. Peter's low point comes with his denial of Jesus during the trial, as reported in all the gospels. At least he was trying to follow Jesus from afar off, whereas all the other disciples had already run away. But it all proved too much for him and he denied Jesus three times – something that he bitterly regretted.

But it is Peter who first realised that Jesus was the Messiah, and after the Ascension and Pentecost, it is Peter who became the natural leader of the disciples, as reported in the Acts of the Apostles. The first 12 chapters of Acts describe how Peter became the leader. He was the one that got up to address the crowds, as reported in Acts Chapter 2. Many of the apostles perform healing miracles, but it is Peter who again takes the lead in this.

We do not know for sure what eventually happened to Peter, but tradition has it that he ended up in Rome in the early 60s CE where he was martyred.

James and his younger brother, **John,** were the sons of Zebedee. Jesus gave them the name **Boanergies,** which means Sons of Thunder. As stated above, they were also part of the inner circle and close to Jesus. It would seem, however, that there were times when these brothers were none too popular with the rest of the disciples. Mark Chapter 10, verses 35 – 45 describes how the brothers came together and asked Jesus whether they could sit one on Jesus' right hand and one on Jesus' left hand, when it came to the Kingdom of Glory. They lost out on this because Jesus then explained patiently that this was not for him to grant.

When the ten heard about this, they became indignant with James and John. (Mark 10: 41).

I don't wonder – why should they have special treatment! The story is repeated in Matthew Chapter 20, verses 20 – 27, only in this account their scheming mother made the request on their behalf. I am sure that didn't help either!

We know little about James, sometimes known as James the Elder or James the Greater. According to Acts 12 verse 2, James was the first of the disciples to be martyred by being put to death with the sword by King Herod. John is probably the "disciple whom Jesus loved", or "that other disciple" in John's Gospel. This adds to the possibility that John was the author of the fourth gospel, as stated in Chapter 2. By tradition, John is often thought as being a little younger than the other disciples, or, at any rate, he seems to have been fitter than Peter, as we can see from John's Gospel when the disciples had just received the news that Jesus' tomb was empty:

So Peter and the other disciple (that is, probably, John) *started for the tomb. Both were running, but the other disciple outran Peter and reached the tomb first. He bent over and looked in at the strips of linen lying there but did not go in. Then Simon Peter, who was behind him, arrived and went into the tomb.* (John 20: 3 – 6).

This is my evidence for supposing that Peter was quite a large man and perhaps none too fit, whereas, the younger John was leaner and fitter. But it is Peter who is the leader and is prepared to go into the tomb.

In the first chapters of the Acts, John is often bracketed with Peter, and they worked together, but again it is Peter who is the leader. There is no record of the death of John, but tradition has it that, unlike the other disciples, he lived to extreme old age in Ephesus, finally dying about the year 100 C.E. much revered and respected by all.

Andrew was the brother of Simon Peter. Together they were the first disciples to be chosen by Jesus, according to all three Synoptic Gospels. But in John's Gospel, Andrew is the first to find Jesus and he immediately goes off and calls his brother, Simon Peter.

The first thing Andrew did was to find his brother Simon and tell him, "We have found the Messiah" (that is the Christ). And he brought him to Jesus. (John 1: 41 – 42.).

This is probably the greatest action of his life. He was also the disciple who found the lad with the five loaves and two fishes when the five thousand were fed. He was probably the elder brother and there is no evidence that the prominence of his younger brother, Peter, rankled in any way. We know nothing more about Andrew but his main claim to fame was that he was the first disciple and was responsible for introducing his brother, Peter, to Jesus.

Philip is always the fifth disciple in any of the lists of the disciples. Philip appears occasionally in John's Gospel and seems to have been a faithful follower:

Philip said, "Lord show us the Father and that will be enough for us." (John 14: 8).

He then receives quite a ticking off from Jesus:

Jesus answered: "Don't you know me, Philip, even after I have been among you quite a long time? How can you say, 'Show us the Father'? Don't you know that I am in the Father, and the Father is in me?...." (John 14: 9 – 10).

However, it is Philip who is responsible for bringing **Bartholomew** or **Nathanael** to Jesus. There is a slight mystery here because Nathanael does not appear in the Synoptic Gospels and Bartholomew does not appear in John's Gospel. It is generally assumed that Bartholomew and Nathanael are the same man. Anyway, we have something of a character here, because Bartholomew/Nathanael clearly does not think much of Nazareth:

Philip found Nathanael and told him, "We have found the one Moses wrote about in the Law, and about whom the prophets also wrote – Jesus of Nazareth, son of Joseph." "Nazareth! Can anything good come from there?" Nathanael asked. "Come and see," said Philip. When Jesus saw Nathanael approaching, he said of him, "Here is a true Israelite, in whom there is nothing false." (John 1: 45 – 47).

Bartholomew/Nathanael appears to have been a man who spoke his mind, but Jesus saw a lot in him.

Thomas we have come across before in Chapter 7. He was the one who had serious doubts after the Resurrection, but in the end all was well.

Matthew or **Levi** was one disciple who was probably quite wealthy. He sat by the side of the road at the tax collector's booth and in Mark Chapter 2, Jesus asked Levi to get up and follow him, which Levi did. Afterwards, Levi entertained Jesus to dinner at his house where many tax collectors and "sinners" were also eating. Tax collectors were very unpopular and the haughty Pharisees were naturally very dismissive of this. Matthew is not mentioned after his call, but he is credited with giving up his "business" to follow Jesus. It used to be thought that he was the author of Matthew's Gospel, but, to-day, scholars think this is most unlikely.

Judas Iscariot is the disciple who betrayed Jesus. He arrived in the Garden of Gethsemane, with a crowd armed with swords and clubs, pointed Jesus out with the result that Jesus was arrested, and this lead to the trial and Crucifixion. According to Matthew's Gospel, Judas became so full of remorse that he went away and hanged himself. It remains something of a mystery as to why Jesus chose Judas in the first place, and then why did Judas become such a traitor? One possible explanation is that Judas became impatient that Jesus was not turning out as Judas had expected and so he turned against Jesus.

Finally we come to **James,** son of Alphaeus, **Thaddeus** and **Simon** the Zealot. Instead of Thaddeus, Luke's list has **Judas** son of James. We know next to nothing about any of these disciples. They appear to just make up the numbers. The James is sometimes known as James the Less – to me an unfortunate title, but it is to distinguish him from James the Greater. There are at least three James' mentioned in the New Testament: James the Greater and James the Less should not be confused with James, the brother of Jesus, who is mentioned from time to time but was not a disciple.

****

Finally, we come to **Paul.** He was the first and greatest theologian and missionary in the early years of Christianity. It was he, more than any of the 12 disciples, who was responsible for spreading the Good News about Jesus to the world outside Jerusalem and Galilee. After Jesus Christ, more books have been written about Paul than about anyone else during this period.

However, Paul was not one of the 12 and in fact he never met Jesus before the Resurrection. He turns out to be very different from Peter and the other disciples. He was born sometime during the early years of the first century, perhaps about 5 C.E. in Tarsus in Cilicia in what is to-day the south coast of modern Turkey. He was a Jew, but also, unusually for a Jew, a Roman citizen. Unlike the 12 disciples, he was well educated probably at the University of Athens and also possibly in Jerusalem. Acts 18: 3 states that Paul was by profession a tentmaker. In his early years, he was a Pharisee, and violently opposed to the Christians and all they represented. He was present at the stoning to death of Stephen, the first Christian martyr, where he had his original name of Saul:

And Saul was there giving approval to his (Stephen's) *death.* (Acts 8: 1).

In fact the young Saul at this stage became ever more passionate in his persecution of Christians:

But Saul began to destroy the church. Going from house to house, he dragged off men and women and put them in prison. (Acts 8: 3).

Meanwhile, Saul was still breathing out murderous threats against the Lord's disciples. He went out to the high priest and asked him for letters to the synagogues in Damascus, so that if he found any there who belonged to the Way, whether men or women, he might take them as prisoners to Jerusalem. (Acts 9: 1 – 2).

Not a nice man! Acts Chapter 9 then goes on to describe the well-known conversion of Saul on the road to Damascus, where he was rendered speechless and blind for three days. Saul never did anything by halves. After this, from being an arch persecutor of Christians, Saul turned into a passionate and outspoken missionary of the Christian message. The book of Acts goes on to describe in some detail the three missionary journeys that Saul undertook with various friends to different parts of what is to-day Turkey and Greece. It was on the first Missionary journey when Saul and Barnabas, his companion, were in Cyprus that he began to be called Paul. Acts 9: 13 refers to "Saul, who is also called Paul". Saul/Paul remained passionate in his Evangelism and had a hard time with some of his visits, but even after prison visits and floggings, he pressed on regardless. His big ambition was to get to Rome, which he succeeded in doing in the closing chapters of Acts. His final journey to Rome included an alarming shipwreck off the island of Malta, which is vividly described in Acts Chapter 27. Needless to say, Paul, although technically a prisoner in the ship, took charge. The chapter finishes with one of the most dramatic passages in the New Testament. The ship had become stuck fast on a sand-bar:

The soldiers planned to kill the prisoners to prevent any of them from swimming away and escaping. But the centurion wanted to spare Paul's life and kept them from carrying out their plan. He ordered those who could swim to jump overboard first to get to land. The rest were to get there on planks or on pieces of the ship. In this way everyone reached land in safety. (Acts 27: 42 – 44).

After further adventures on Malta, Paul did finally reach Rome under guard. There he was allowed to remain for two years in a rented house in comparative peace and he was able to welcome all who came to see him. At this stage Acts breaks off the narrative and we do not know for sure the final stages of Paul's life. But we do know that he was executed in Rome sometime in the 60s C.E. Some scholars think that he may have had time for further travels but this seems unlikely.

Paul was a great letter writer and many of his letters are given in the New Testament. In Chapter 2, I described which letters were almost certainly written by Paul and which letters, still full of good Christian values, were probably not written by Paul, although ascribed to him.

Earlier I described my vision of how I imagined Peter to be: a large man, impetuous, and not the most intellectual. Paul appears to me to be rather the opposite: a small man, physically not very strong, but full of energy and restless. Paul does actually mean "the little one". And there is evidence that his health was not good:

To keep me from becoming conceited because of these surpassing great revelations, there was given me a thorn in my flesh, a messenger of Satan, to torment me. Three times I pleaded with the Lord to take it away from me. But he said to me, "My grace is sufficient for you, for my power is made perfect in weakness." Therefore I will boast all the more gladly about my weaknesses, so that Christ's power may rest on me. That is why, for Christ's sake, I delight in weaknesses, in insults, in hardships, in persecutions, in difficulties. For when I am weak, then I am strong. (II Corinthians 12: 7 – 10).

Quite what his physical infirmity was we do not know. But there were traditions that he was short, bow legged and bald.

This is how he has been depicted in some early Byzantine paintings. He also appears to have had poor eyesight and possible evidence for this comes from Paul's Epistle to the Galatians:

See what large letters I use as I write to you with my own hand! (Galatians 6: 11).

Furthermore Paul admits to an illness in Galatians 4: 13 when he first preached to the Galatians. This may have been some form of epilepsy and it could also explain why he became more and more dependent on the physician Luke to keep him going, as I mentioned in Chapter 2.

An example of Paul being totally out of step with modern thinking comes in his first letter to the Corinthians:

"Women should remain silent in the churches. They are not allowed to speak, but must be in submission, as the law says. If they want to enquire about something, they should ask about their own husbands at home; for it is disgraceful for a woman to speak in the church." (1 Corinthians 14: 34 – 35).

This, of course, is totally unacceptable in this day and age, but it was quite normal 2000 years ago, and if Paul wrote this, he was a man of his time. It is, however, now thought that a later scribe inserted these verses into Paul's letter, but it still gives us a good idea of contemporary thought. There is a similar "forgery" in 1 Timothy 2: 11 – 15, where women are encouraged to be quiet, submissive and childbearing, but then, as stated in Chapter 2, this Epistle is probably not original Paul.

There are also problems relating to Paul and the subject of homosexuality which will be dealt with in the next chapter.

It really does seem that at times Paul could be thoroughly difficult, manipulative, argumentative and given to outbursts of rage towards his enemies. Thus it is hardly surprising that there is some evidence that Paul and Peter did not get on that well if, again, we study what has become known as the "Incident at Antioch" in Paul's Epistle to the Galatians:

When Peter came to Antioch, I opposed him to his face, because he was clearly in the wrong. Before certain men came from James, he used to eat with the Gentiles. But when they arrived, he began to draw back and separate himself from the Gentiles because he was afraid of those who belonged to the circumcision group. The other Jews joined him in his hypocrisy, so that by their hypocrisy even Barnabas was led astray. (Galatians 2: 11 – 13).

And yet, there was another side to Paul: he had many friends whom he dearly loved, and at times he went out of his way to send them his love and greetings. An example of this is the last chapter of the Epistle to the Romans, which is spent almost entirely in passing on his greetings to various "dear friends".

As a little aside, and before we finish with Paul, it might appear that by his standards, even a little alcohol would be treated as a sin. Happily, all is not lost for in his first letter to his friend, Timothy, Paul (or the writer of I Timothy) writes one of my favourite verses in the Bible:

Stop drinking only water, and use a little wine because of your stomach and your frequent illnesses. (1 Tim. 5: 23).

So, Paul could be a thoroughly disagreeable man at times, but then it is often these sorts of people who can in the end succeed more fully and get things done. There is much more that could be written about Paul, and for the interested reader, there are any number of books that can be read on the subject. But the important thing to understand is that it was Paul who was the first to understand fully the death and Resurrection of Jesus and then **to spread the Gospel to the Gentile world.**

Chapter 9:
Christianity and Other
Great Religions

Over the past 5,000 or so years there have been seven main world religions. In order of time from when they started, they are:

1. **Hinduism**
2. **Buddhism**
3. **Judaism**
4. **Christianity**
5. **Islam**
6. **Sikhism**
7. **Bahá'i Faith**

From each of these seven there have been dozens of off-shoots, or different sects, which need not concern us too much. But a very basic understanding of what each of these religions stand for can help us with our Christian religion, and also help to see why there has been so much conflict between peoples of different religions. Ignorance of other religions can be a cause of much misunderstanding and prejudice. This in turn is potentially dangerous and at its worst leads to war, as, sadly, we have seen all too often over the centuries. To-day, there is still far too much conflict, and we are currently witnessing a rise of religious intolerance in the Middle East. Very broadly, the great religions of the world can be divided into two main groups: the three Abrahamic religions, that is Judaism, Christianity and Islam, who all trace their origins back to Abraham, and the remaining religions that generally originate from the Indian subcontinent. In the earlier days, these religions were highly localised. This means that if you were born in a certain area, you were most likely to adhere to the religion of that region, at least to start with. To-day, most religions are much more widespread.

Before we look at each of these religions, it is helpful to see what tends to make a religion, and broadly, I would suggest the following:

1. A unified set of beliefs.

2. A unifying set of practices or ritual. These could include prayer, meditation, pilgrimage, chanting, singing and dance as in the Whirling Dervishes whom we will come to later.

3. Reports of some mystical experience, for example Jesus and the Resurrection in Christianity, or Mohammed and his encounter with Allah in Islam.

4. Provision of comfort especially in times of suffering and death.

5. Attempts to explain some of the mysteries of life.

As for the unified set of beliefs, many religions have in common a belief in a God or gods and then a general instruction to be nice to other human beings. This can be summed up in the two greatest commandments as given in Matthew's Gospel:

One of them (a Pharisee), *an expert in the law, tested him* (Jesus) *with this question: "Teacher, which is the greatest commandment in the Law?" Jesus replied, "'Love the Lord your God with all your heart and with all your soul and with all your mind.'" This is the first and greatest commandment. And the second is like it: 'Love your neighbour as yourself.' All the Law and the Prophets hang on these two commandments."* (Matt. 22: 35 – 40).

In a nutshell, the idea is to love God and then show love and respect to all people on Earth. This is the Christian religion. The other six main religions all say much the same thing in their own way, although not all of them have God.

What follows will be a very brief description of the seven main religions without any attempt to go into any great detail. After all, whole books have been written on each of them including their often complicated history.

1. Hinduism.

Hinduism is the oldest living religion in the world because elements of it stretch back several thousand years. It is the third largest religion to-day after Christianity and Islam, having some 900 million adherents worldwide. The majority of the people of India (some 80%) and also Nepal regard themselves as Hindu. Unlike most other religions, Hinduism has no single founder, no single scripture and not even a commonly agreed set of teachings. However, Hindus do believe in a Supreme God, from whom a multitude of different deities come. Most Hindus believe in one of three principal deities, Shiva, Vishnu or Shakti. Thus Hinduism is a *polytheistic* religion in contrast to most other religions which are *monotheistic*, having just one God. It is a rigid and hard system that believes that human beings are not all born equal. Thus there was a system of four *castes* that determined one's position in society. At the top were the *Brahmins* who were the priests and the teachers. Below the four castes were the untouchables who did all the dirty work. Most Hindus believe firmly in the existence of an enduring soul that moves from one body to another at death, or the cycle of birth, death and rebirth. This is known as the process of *re-incarnation*. All this is governed by *Karma* whereby if you lead a good life, you can hope to re-incarnate in your next life in a higher caste. Thus your next incarnation is always dependent on how you got on in your previous life. If you lead a bad life, then you are in trouble because you might return as an untouchable or even as an animal! Thus there is a strong incentive to lead a good life and behave yourself. Hinduism also emphasises the importance of finding a "Guru" or teacher who can impart real knowledge.

The ultimate aim of a devout Hindu is that after very many lives, one hopes to reach a state of *nirvana* or eternal bliss, whereupon no more arduous lives on Earth would be necessary.

2. Buddhism.

Buddhism came into being during the time when Hinduism was already going strong, with the birth of a man destined to be the "Buddha" in about 485 BCE. He was born as a prince of a small territory in what is now called Nepal, although he was ethnically an Indian. He was raised in splendid comfort but no amount of material pleasure could satisfy the young man. At the age of 29, he left the palace to search for a deeper meaning to life in secluded forests and remote mountains. Despite a great struggle, he found nothing until at the age of 35, when one night during a full moon, he sat beneath a large pipal tree known as the Bodhi tree at Bodh Gaya in deep and tranquil meditation, thinking about the hidden meanings of the mind, the universe and life. He gained the supreme Enlightenment experience or *nirvana* and from that time on he was known as "the Buddha". This Enlightenment was not a revelation from some divine being, but consisted of an all-embracing insight into the nature of mind and all phenomena. It meant that the Buddha was no longer subject to craving, ill-will and delusion, but rather he had acquired an unshakeable peace and a complete end to all forms of inner suffering. Having realized the goal of Perfect Enlightenment, the Buddha spent the next 45 years as a supreme teacher and philosopher. He lived to be over 80 and many of the images of him show a man of considerable weight sitting in a lotus position, completely serene. Other images show him in a recumbent position, again quite serene. To-day, Buddhism is the fourth largest religion in the world with over 350 million followers. The religion is practised mainly in India, Thailand and other parts of the Far East.

It is not possible here to go into the full teachings of the Buddha. But in a nutshell, he taught that all forms of being, human and otherwise, are afflicted with suffering and that the cause of this suffering is "craving". As with Hinduism, at the end of one's life, one returns again with another life and this cycle goes on and on until one eventually achieves *nirvana*. What happens then is not clear, but the Buddha taught that one should concentrate on one's day to day life and not worry about what happens afterwards.

The five Buddhist Precepts of what not to do, go well with the "Thou shalt nots" of Christianity's Ten Commandments, (see Exodus Chapter 20). You should not:

1. Deliberately cause the death of any living being.

2. Intentionally take the property of another for one's own.

3. Indulge in sexual misconduct, in particular adultery.

4. Lie and break promises.

5. Drink alcohol; or take stupefying drugs which lead to lack of mindfulness.

Buddhists do not believe in one Supreme Being. In Buddhist cosmology, our present universe, from the moment of the "Big Bang" up until now, some 13.8 billion years, is but one among countless millions of universes. (Incidentally, the age of the Universe turns out to be close to three times the age of the earth, see Chapter 1). The Buddha gave an estimate of the age of a single universe cycle of around 37 billion years, which sounds a remarkably good "estimate" given what we now know from modern cosmology.

Rather similar to Buddhism is **Jainism.** This was started in the sixth century BCE by a prince named Mahavira, born about 599 BCE. Jainism has many of the beliefs of Buddhism but is more extreme in that it believes that *nirvana* could be achieved more quickly by extreme self-denial. Thus adherents are encouraged to become a monk or a nun, not to kill or hurt any living being or animal. They are strictly vegetarian and not allowed to swat even an insect or mosquito! They are discouraged from eating vegetables, but they are allowed fruit that has fallen to the ground. It is a life of extreme non-violence. Jainism is not a world religion, but it has had influence and there are still millions of adherents living in India to-day.

All in all, Buddhism has much to commend it. Many of its ideas fit in well with Christianity. Differences start to occur when one considers what may happen after this life. But the Buddha, sitting comfortably in his lotus position, appears wonderfully SERENE!

3. Judaism.

Judaism or the Jewish religion was founded by Moses around 1500 years BCE although all Jews trace their history back to Isaac and Abraham. The Jewish religion started with God's "Covenant" with Abraham, and was cemented when he gave Moses and the children of Israel the Ten Commandments, as given in the Old Testament book of Exodus, Chapter 20. As stated in Chapter 2 of this book, the first five books of the

Christian Bible, known as the Torah, are central to the Jewish Faith. Most of the Ten Commandments are unexceptional, about not stealing, not committing murder and so on. A group of people could come up with these instructions easily enough with or without a god. It is the first Commandment that is exceptional:

"You shall have no other gods before me."   (Exodus 20: 2).

At the time, this was an exceptional belief not shared by any other religion. Jews firmly believe in one God with whom they have a "Covenant", based on the Law expressed in the first five books of the Old Testament. They also believe that there are no other gods. Furthermore, God cannot be subdivided into different persons, so this is where they differ from the Christian view of God, who is God the Father, God the Son, or Jesus Christ, and God the Holy Spirit, referred to as the "Trinity", which I will mention in the next section. They accept that Jesus existed as a man and was crucified, but they do not believe in the Resurrection nor do they believe that he was the Messiah. They believe that God is omnipotent, omnipresent and beyond time, which means that he has always existed and always will exist. He is also "Transcendent" which means that he is above and beyond all earthly things, merciful and forgiving.

Jews worship in a building called a synagogue, and each spiritual leader is called a "Rabbi" which means a teacher. To-day, there are male and female Rabbis. Currently there are about 13.5 million Jewish people in the world, living mainly in the U.S.A. and Israel. Before and during World War II, some 6 million Jews were murdered by Nazi Germany in the Holocaust. All religions have been persecuted from time to time in history, but the persecution of the Jews during World War II is arguably the greatest evil of all time. This had, and continues to have, a profound effect on the Jewish people.   In 1948, the state of Israel was set up to include part of Jerusalem as their Holy City, but sadly, this has led to a continuing source of conflict with Arab nations, who also believe that Jerusalem is their Holy City.

One of the main attributes of Judaism is its warmth and love of family. They also have a high appreciation of educational scholarship. I have happy memories of teaching a number of Jewish boys many of whom were excellent students with very supportive parents. On one occasion my wife and I were honoured to be invited to the Bar Mitzvah of a 13 year old pupil. The Bar Mitzvah is a coming of age ritual whereby the boy is recognised by Jewish tradition as having the same rights as a full grown man. He becomes morally and ethically responsible for his decisions and actions. There was a large contingent of extended family present who were all obviously devoted to the boy. There is a similar ritual for girls when aged 12 called a "Bat Mitzvah."

As with other religions Judaism can be practised in different ways and with varying interpretations put on Biblical Old Testament texts. Some are "Orthodox" which in practice means they often keep very much to themselves with their own schools and institutions. They observe more of the laws many of which come from the first five books of the Bible, this being easier to do if they spend most of their time together. Others are less orthodox or "liberal" and more prepared to integrate into society.

4. Christianity.

Christianity goes back to the time of Jesus Christ whose teaching began about the year 30 CE. Over the years, the Christian Church has had a lot to answer for. In historical times, the Church has been seen to be the ultimate control freak: "unless you toe the line and do as we say, then you are in for hellfire and damnation." We need not go into all the iniquities of the Spanish Inquisition and the brutal punishments that were dished out for heresy and blasphemy in Mediaeval times whereby belief was enforced on pain of punishment and torture up to and including death. On a more domestic level, even in Victorian times, in a typical country village Anglican Church, the Lord of the Manor sat in a high status pew, while the servants were expected to sit at the back of the church out of the way. One trouble is that this hangover from terrible events from the past has turned away so many otherwise well-meaning and spiritual people. The position has improved greatly over the past 50 years or so, but there are still problems. To many young people, the Church is still seen to be irrelevant, sexist and homophobic, but then, to be fair, so are some of the other religions mentioned in this chapter. In the Anglican Church, the sexist position is a lot better than it was and there are now many excellent women priests and indeed women bishops. The "Gay Issue" is more complicated and I shall return to this in Chapter 10. All Christian Churches believe firmly in the doctrine of the Trinity, that is, God the Father, God the Son, who is Jesus Christ, and God the Holy Spirit. The main point about Christianity is that Christians believe that Jesus Christ was the Son of God and that he came into the world to save us from our sins. Many of the other religions recognise Jesus as a great prophet, teacher and even healer, but they do not see him as God's Son. The legacy from the Jewish religion is the idea of one God only and no other gods, from the first Commandment. In fact apart from the Trinity, many of the Christian beliefs come straight from Judaism.

The Anglican Church is just one part of the Christian Church. There are two other major branches that we need to mention briefly: the **Roman Catholic Church** and the **Russian** or **Eastern Orthodox Church.** The Roman Catholic Church goes right back to the time of Jesus Christ almost 2000 years ago. There are more than a billion Catholics spread throughout the world but found especially in Southern Europe, the United States, Central and South America and the Philippines, and it is thus the largest church in Christianity. Catholics believe that that the head of the Catholic Church, the Pope, is in direct line of succession from St Peter, and that the Pope has supreme authority. This means that the Pope can speak with infallibility on matters of faith and morals. (As an Anglican, this is something that I find particularly difficult to accept, although in practice he seldom uses it to-day). All priests have to be men who are unmarried, that is unless they are already married men who have converted from another faith. The Catholic Church has a very hierarchical nature with the Pope at the top of the pyramid, followed by cardinals, archbishops, bishops, priests, deacons and laity. When the Pope dies or retires, it is the cardinals who assemble in a conclave to decide which one of them becomes the next Pope. There are three doctrinal issues where the Catholic Church is particularly strong:

1. Their devotion to the Blessed Virgin Mary, Jesus' mother. Catholics believe that Mary herself was immaculately conceived, and this is called the Immaculate Conception. They also believe that she gave birth to Jesus without having sex first. Furthermore she remained a virgin all her life; and finally, her body and soul were raised into heaven. We discussed the topic of the Virgin Birth in Chapter 5.

2. The Catholic Church remains resolutely opposed to all artificial means of contraception. In practice many Catholics totally ignore this, but it does have vast implications especially in the poorer parts of the world. As an Anglican, this is one belief I cannot support.

3. The Catholic Church is resolutely opposed to abortion being the taking of life. Here, I would be more in sympathy with this doctrine but will return to the topic in Chapter 10.

In England, the Roman Catholic Church held sway until the reign of King Henry VIII. He then fell out with the Pope in a big way, because the Pope would not allow him to divorce his first wife, Catherine of Aragon. Henry was in no mood to put up with this, so he cut England off from the Catholic Church, and declared his independence. Thus the new Anglican Church came into existence about 1530 with Henry himself as the head of it. He then proceeded to divorce the unfortunate Catherine so that he could marry his second wife, Anne Boleyn. All this was in order for Henry to father a male heir, which, as it turned out, Anne Boleyn was unable to provide either.

In the matter of divorce, there is a certain irony here. Officially the English Church is against the marriage of divorced people in church, and this has been strictly the case until quite recently. In practice, the rules are generally becoming more and more liberal here, and many clergy do marry divorcées in church, provided he or she thinks the couple suitably sincere. However, the Church of England only came into being because Henry VIII wanted his own way and have a divorce!

The third main Christian religion is the Eastern or Russian Orthodox Church. For the first seven or eight hundred years after Jesus, the Christian Church throughout the east and west remained in relative harmony with the Pope as its head. Then the Eastern Churches began to break away, with the final split with Rome coming about with the Great Schism of 1054.   The Eastern Churches could not accept the papal claim to supreme authority, so they went their own way.   Around 200 million people call themselves Orthodox. Their leaders are referred to as Patriarchs, who can be seen having flowing robes and long beards. They include the churches of Turkey, Russia, Serbia, Romania, Bulgaria, Georgia, Cyprus, Greece, Poland, Albania, the Czech and Slovak lands and, as recently as 1970, the Orthodox Church of America was formed. The nominal head of the Eastern Orthodox Church is the Patriarch of Constantinople. They lay greater emphasis on fasting, prayer and monasticism, but otherwise their beliefs agree broadly with the Anglican Churches.

Finally, a brief word about **Evangelical** Christians including among others Pentecostalists and Non-conformists. These are branches of the Anglican Church that started up around the 18th century. Evangelists believe passionately in the Bible, and often in every word of the Bible. They have a great belief in spreading the "Word" far and wide, and often do a wonderful job.

As with all religions, there is a great deal more that could be written about the Anglican Church, the Catholic Church, the Orthodox Church and the Non-Conformist Churches.

5. Islam.

Followers of Islam are called Muslims. Islam is now the second largest religion in the world after Christianity with some 1.6 billion adherents, and is growing fast. Like Jews and Christians, Muslims firmly believe that there is only one God whom they refer to as Allah. They believe that God sent a number of prophets to mankind to teach them how to live according to his Law. These included Abraham, Moses, Elijah, Elisha and Jesus. The last of these prophets was Muhammad who was born about 570 CE. It is worth noting that they fully accept the existence of Jesus, as one of the prophets sent by God. However, they do not believe in the Crucifixion and Resurrection to eternal life of Jesus, nor that he was the Son of God or Allah. Although Jesus appeared to be crucified, Muslims believe that he did not actually die on the cross. Interestingly, Islam does believe in the Virgin Birth for Jesus. Muslims believe that Islam (that is, a life lived totally in obedience to God's revealed will as taught by all God's prophets) has always existed, but Islam based on the Qur'an (*Note the correct spelling*) and Muhammad dates from the seventh century.

When Muhammad was aged about 40, Muslims believe that the Angel Gabriel appeared to him with a series of revelations from God. The result was that Muhammad recited various verses which were memorised by some of his followers and then written down by others, for Muhammad himself could not write. From then on until he died in the year 632 CE, he experienced intermittently a series of revelations from Allah which he then conveyed to the people. The final result is what we have to-day as the Qur'an. There is quite a lot in the Qur'an about Abraham and Moses. In particular, instead of concentrating upon Isaac, who was Abraham's son by his wife Sarah, and from whom the Children of Israel or the Jews claim descent, Muslims concentrate upon Ishmael. This was the son that Abraham had with Hagar, who was Sarah's servant and whom she gave to Abraham as a second wife so that they could have children. (For a long time Abraham and Sarah did not have children and Isaac was only finally born when Abraham and Sarah were very old). Thus it is through Ishmael that all Muslims trace their connection to Abraham. Jesus is mentioned with due reverence and there is a surprising amount about the Virgin Mary, in fact more than there is in all the Christian New Testament!

Muslims believe in the five Principal Practices of Islam. These are:

1. There is no god save Allah, and Muhammad is his messenger.

2. There shall be ritual prayer five times a day facing in the direction of the Ka'ba in Mecca.

3. Muslims should make money circulate from those with a surplus to those in need.

4. Muslims should fast during the month of Ramadan.

5. Each adult Muslim should go on a major pilgrimage to Mecca at least once in their lifetime lasting five days, if their health permits and if they can afford to pay the costs whilst still discharging their family duties. This is known as the "Hajj".

Mecca is located in Saudi Arabia and is the holiest city in Islam, and also the birthplace of Muhammad. In Mecca there is the Sacred Mosque wherein the Ka'ba, a cuboid structure, is situated at the centre. This is the most sacred point within the most Sacred Mosque and it is known as the "House of God". It contains the Black Stone, which is located externally in one corner of the Ka'ba. It is possible that this may once have been a meteorite but Muslims hold that it was "sent by God" to be included in the building. When pilgrims arrive at Mecca, they then circumambulate the Ka'ba seven times as a symbol of their devotion to God.

As with Judaism and indeed other faiths, there are different ways of practising Islam some of which relate to cultural issues rather than religious practice. The two major branches are **Sunni**, some 85% of the world's Muslims and **Shi'a**, the remaining 15%. Within these, there are diverse schools of theology and law. Through the centuries, the Sunni and Shi'a Muslims have lived side by side in relative harmony in the Middle East. The present unrest between the two is an aberration.

Finally, Islamic mystics are called **Sufis.** They are found amongst both Sunni and Shi'a Muslims and their way of life is Islam, but they emphasise the mystical dimensions. The Sufis trace their origins back to a group of people who sat on a bench in Muhammad's mosque in Medina and were taught the mystical way by Muhammad himself. Thus Sufism is a mystical way of approaching the Islamic faith. They live a life of self-control, dedication to mystical practice, self-purification and thus drawing closer to God. The well-known "Whirling Dervishes" are mainly Turkish Sufis who practise spinning round at what appears to be an alarming rate, with the aim of achieving a form of religious ecstasy. The Sufis in general can be seen to be a powerful antidote to some of the fanatical extremists of Islam.

At the present time there is a problem with the peoples' perceptions of Islam because so many people in the West consider Muslims as strange, foreign and fanatical, and possibly linked to terrorist events. Of course there have been some dreadful terrorist events in recent years, carried out by people claiming to be Muslims, of which the attack on the World Trade Centre on what has come to be known as "9/11" is the most famous and shocking. These terrorists are far removed from what Muhammad and the Qur'an teach. They were using Islam as a cover for these atrocities, and they were trying to set up what they call the Islamic State. The vast majority of Muslims wish to have nothing to do with these events, or with the warped reasoning that accompanies them. In September 2014, more than 120 Muslim Scholars from around the world got together and composed what has become known as the "Letter to Baghdadi".[1] This was an open letter to Abu Bakr al-Baghdadi, the leader of the Islamic State of Iraq and Syria, which, when it was presented in Washington D.C. by Nihad Awad of the Council on American Islamic Relations, said:

"You have misinterpreted Islam into a religion of harshness, brutality, torture and murder." "This is a great wrong and an offense to Islam, to Muslims and to the entire world."

This was essentially addressed to potential radicals in an attempt to dissuade them from joining the ranks of the Islamic State of Iraq and Syria.

Amongst many injunctions, the letter makes clear:

1. It is forbidden in Islam to kill the innocent.

2. It is forbidden in Islam to harm or mistreat - in any way - Christians or "Any people of the Scripture".

Islam is essentially a religion of peace that rejects all forms or terrorism:

True servants of the Merciful are those who walk humbly on the earth and say "Peace!" to the ignorant who accost them. (Qur'an Chapter 25, verse 64).

The Qur'an is also clear that there should be no compulsion in matters of religion:

---

[1] See www.lettertobaghdadi.com.

There shall be no compulsion in religion.   (Qur'an Chapter 2, verse 256).

I believe this last to be true for all religions, including Christianity: there should never be any coercion to join any religion.

What we have to do in the West is to try to put an end to the violence, fear and hatred throughout many parts of the world. One way forward might be to extend the hand of friendship to moderate and peaceful Muslims throughout the world. This is well worth doing in its own right, but sadly it will have no effect on the violent extremists who hate the moderate Muslims, and indeed followers of all the other religions. I am pessimistic here and fear that militant extremism is going to be with us for many years to come.

6. Sikhism

Sikhism is one of the world's youngest religions being founded by Guru Nanak (1469 – 1539) in the 16th century. It started in the Punjab region of what is now India and Pakistan. Despite being only being about 500 years old, it is the world's fifth largest religion with over 20 million followers, after, in order of size, Christianity, Islam, Hinduism and Buddhism. Sikhism is a monotheistic religion, (that is believing in one God) and it stresses the importance of good actions rather than merely carrying out rituals. Like many other religions, it stresses the importance of honesty, hard work, serving others and being generous to the less fortunate. Unlike some other eastern religions, they do not believe in fasting, the caste system, or in abstinence from alcohol, smoking and drugs.

Sikhs do not cut their hair, with the result that it grows very long. This is one reason why Sikh men wear turbans to keep the hair tidy. Sikh women wear a turban or a scarf.

7. Bahá'i Faith

The Bahá'i faith is another of the world's younger religions. It was founded by Bahá'u'lláh in Iran in 1863. There are some 6 million followers in the world including about 6,000 in the U.K. The Bahá'i religion is unusual in that it accepts all other faiths as being true and valid. Thus it accepts the divine nature of the missions of, among others, Abraham, Moses, Buddha, Jesus and the Prophet Muhammed. These were all prophets or messengers (called Divine Messengers) of which Bahá'u'lláh is the most recent one. There may well be others still to come. The Bahá'is believe in a single God who is omnipotent, omniscient, imperishable and perfect in every way. They believe that God is too great to be ever understood by the human mind. All we can hope to do is to believe that God exists. They believe in the unity of God, the unity of religion and the unity of humanity. The central idea is thus one of unity: we should all work together for the common benefit of humanity.

What I like about the Bahá'i religion is that it is very tolerant of all other religions, which is why I have included a brief mention of it here. I have met a number of Bahá'i followers at Interfaith Forums and they all strike me as being far sighted and tolerant. However, one big difference with Christianity is that they do not believe that God has, or will ever, become incarnate as a human being. However, similar to Islam, Jesus remains one of the great prophets.

****

As stated earlier, Judaism, Christianity and Islam are known as the three Abrahamic religions because they all claim to have been originally started by Abraham. A family tree showing the connection between these religions might be constructed along these lines:

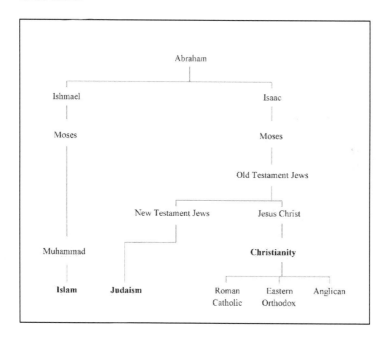

The above tree could be extended downward into the many different strands of the three main religions to-day.

In this chapter, we have looked very briefly at seven of the main religions of the world. There are many other smaller religions that should not be overlooked. I emphasise again what was said earlier in this chapter, that all religions preach the love and respect of other human beings in this world. Surely one might expect these different religions then to come together and act as a unifying force? Unfortunately, the world is not yet ready for this, but progress is being made in this direction if rather unevenly. I believe very strongly in finding a way forward from this confusion. In some areas, "Interfaith" groups have started up with pockets of forward minded and well-meaning people from many different faiths, who have been prepared to meet up with one another. They then need to get to know one another and talk to each other. This is important, because strangers just being polite to one another, although well-meaning, are not likely to make much progress. The important thing is that they all *listen* to each other and try to understand each other. There will be sharp differences, of course, but there should be no heated arguments, no hostilities and no "grandstanding", that is shouting from a distance. What I am so against is an exclusivist approach to religion, which is exemplified by certain fundamentalist groups both in the Christian religion and in other religions. Just because you do not follow my particular religion, does not mean that you are automatically heading for hellfire and damnation. A good cheerful discussion is excellent, *provided all sides appreciate and understand the differences involved, at the same time showing due respect to other religions present.* I am all for good hearted disagreement punctuated by cheerful bursts of laughter. In this context, the Bahá'i Faith has much to commend it.

****

I return finally to the Church of England and how it is seen in the world to-day. Many congregations of the Church of England are in decline. Rural parishes in England in particular are struggling to keep going with a small team of priests and laity trying to keep up to 15, or even 20 Parish Churches viable. And yet, all is by no means lost. There are selected parishes, which tend to be in more urban and suburban areas, that are flourishing. In my view, for an Anglican Church to succeed, three factors seem to be influential:

1. **Geographical Situation:** In the U.K. the Anglican Church tends to thrive when it is in a relatively urban or suburban reasonably well educated area. A degree of affluence amongst the congregation is often helpful. An alternative is that the church is in an area where there are a good number of Christian immigrants. A good example of this is the Afro-Caribbean community in England. Many Roman Catholic churches in England are also often well attended, partly because of European immigrants. Currently, the Anglican Church is experiencing a particular difficulty in getting into urban working class areas and estates. I see this as a real problem for the Church in the years ahead. I well remember one vicar in a relatively poor area saying to me sadly that it was over two years since he last conducted a wedding in his church. Abroad the position is very mixed: the Anglican Church is thriving in parts of America, and growing strongly in parts of Africa. Interestingly, people in China are also to-day

converting to Christianity in large numbers, in spite of state persecution.

2. **Personnel:** A good vicar is needed. He or she has to be a leader, and a degree of charisma works wonders here. In addition there needs to be a good team of helpers in the congregation to make up effective team of churchwardens, sidesmen and other volunteers supporting the church. These helpers should be prepared to go out of their way to welcome new-comers to the church. There are people who still find some churches to be unwelcoming. Recently, I completed four years serving my local church on the outskirts of London as a churchwarden, and this was a very rewarding and enriching experience. Meeting and greeting anyone who came to the church was always a high priority for me.

3. **Environment:** The church building itself needs to be bright and cheerful giving you a feeling of warmth and welcome as soon as you enter. Some older churches tend to be dark and gloomy places and are simply too big for their congregations. Bright lights and some colourful flowers can obviously help, as can signs of activity, such as children's drawings, posters, photographs and so on.

****

In the 21st century, in my view, the two dominant religions are going to be Christianity and Islam. This is not to belittle the value of all the other religions. But Christians and Muslims, and indeed all religions, need to meet each other and, as stated earlier, offer one another the hand of friendship. In history, so many of our bloodiest and most intense conflicts have been due to religious intolerance.

In conclusion, it is my fervent hope and prayer that one day perhaps towards the end of this century, there will be a wonderful meeting of minds, and reconciliation between all religions. Different religions will still cheerfully exist alongside each other, but they will understand each other so much better and the world may then be a much more peaceful place.

Chapter 10:
Four Difficult Issues.

In this chapter we are going to tackle four really tough issues. They are all issues that Christians should think about carefully. But they come with a health warning: there are no easy answers! That does not, however, mean that we should duck these issues as many try to do. We should examine each of them and at least try to find a way forward. In some cases, there are the two extreme and opposing views both of which are clearly unacceptable, the answer lying somewhere in between. The other thing to realise is that in a democratic society, the consensus of opinion may favour one particular course of action and that is pursued. This does not mean that course of action is necessarily correct!

1. God and the Problem of Evil.

If God is omnipotent, omniscient and benevolent, and if he created and directs this world, why is there so much evil, unpleasantness and suffering? Why do so many people, including believers, have to put up with such miserable lives? Is it the case that, after all, God is not fully omnipotent? It's a good question often asked and no-one, if they are honest, fully knows the answer. It is my belief that it is this one question, more than any other, that has put off more otherwise good and honest people from having a faith. Human suffering has been around at least as long as mankind and seems likely to continue.

We can divide human suffering as coming from at least two very different causes. The first is suffering as a result of natural disasters. The second comes from the dreadful human destruction of life in whole areas of the world as a result of war, genocide and human carelessness. There are some cases where these two merge towards each other. Recent examples of the first cause include the great tsunami of December 2004 that destroyed whole communities along the eastern coasts of India and Sri Lanka, and the floods around the mouth of the river Mississippi in 2005, resulting in large areas of New Orleans being under water. This is because we live on a planet that is still evolving and cooling. From time to time there will be faults in the crust of the Earth, and we must add to that a continually turbulent weather system. It is only a matter of time before the St Andreas fault line in California shifts causing another major earthquake in that area. Hopefully, mankind will be more prepared next time and there will not be the huge loss of life that occurred in the 1906 San Francisco earthquake. There is nothing evil in these natural disasters, but they do sometimes cause great suffering to the people involved. Another well-known catastrophe was the Aberfan disaster on 21 October 1966. On that fateful day a large mass of coal waste slid down a Welsh hillside engulfing a primary school in the village of Aberfan killing 116 children and 28 adults. The hillside was man-made, but the result was the same, and thus this is an example of the two types of cause merging towards each other. Even to-day, more than 50 years later, some survivors remain deeply affected by the event. A much more recent example was the disastrous fire in the Grenfell Tower in West London in June 2017. Some 72 people lost their lives and many more have been made homeless. While this has caused much anguish and ill feeling, there are plenty of examples of how this disaster brought out the best in some people, especially the fire service and rescuers. And there are many other examples that could be quoted.

Suffering can also result from the loss of one or more limbs, as a result of an accident. This is not evil in itself, but it can hardly be described as particularly good for the victim either. If one loses one leg, well, this is very unfortunate, but one must then learn to hop along on the other leg as best as one can.

We turn now to the second cause which is the suffering as a result of manmade war and genocide. It has to be said that some of the greatest evils have been and are committed in the name of religion with people deceiving themselves that they are acting in the name of God or Allah. At the present time, there remains considerable tension and fighting in some parts of the Middle East. Besides the destruction of so many buildings, some very ancient and sacred, bad enough in itself, there is the resultant extreme human misery. We now have a refugee problem with whole families risking their lives sometimes in bad weather in trying to go by sea to Greece and Italy. Many lives have been lost but the people are so desperate to escape the horrors of war.

This is the question that no-one can answer fully. All I can say is this: let us try to imagine a world where there is no evil and suffering. Everyone, presumably, would still go to work, but then after that, one would be free to do as one wished and perhaps enjoy one great long lasting party. This world would have no *challenges* and we would all remain eternally nice to one another. Human beings would remain in the Garden of Eden, in a state of innocence without the knowledge of good and evil. Thus life would become like a paradise on a tropical island such as the Galapagos. Here the tortoises have had an easy existence, and have grown large and indolent. They move slowly and are quite unable to cope when an outside force such as when other animals are introduced to the island. Another example is the moa, a large bird that once existed on New Zealand. It had no predators, and life was good, so it grew larger and larger and then it lost the ability to fly, this being a waste of time and effort. Man arrived several hundred years ago; here was easy meat which had no means of escape and therefore the moa soon became extinct. I realise that this does little to answer the question about God, but we do need some *challenges* to overcome and resist in order to make progress in this life. And if we are able to withstand and conquer evil, then that is a great step forward. The point is that we are here to develop in a *spiritual* sense, and without these challenges from time to time, it would be very difficult to make much progress on the spiritual front. Men came back from the hard fighting on the front line in World Wars I and II, some of whom had suffered terribly, but in many cases, once they were over their trauma, they said that they welcomed the experience, and they had made huge spiritual advances. Having said that, I realise that there were others who took the attitude, "This must never happen again". This is because there were many people including civilians who had suffered terribly and had never got over the experience. They became so traumatised that spiritual development was not possible.

Finally, I have to admit that it continues to bother me greatly that there is just so much extreme pain and misery in this world. What we have to do is to find ways to minimise all this suffering because there is far too much. If we can succeed in doing this, this would also provide room for some spiritual development.

2. The Gay Issue.

This is another really important issue which is one that has turned so many otherwise well-meaning and good people away from the Church. On the one hand, there are some Christians who are amongst the strongest opponents of homosexuality and gay marriage. In many ways the issue of homosexuality has been a purely cultural one, riddled with prejudice and hypocrisy. On the other hand, there are Christians who are amongst the strongest advocates of homosexuality and gay marriage. Thus this one issue has really been so divisive in the past, and although the situation has vastly improved during my lifetime, there are still be strong and bitter divisions. In Chapter 9, I stated that the Church of England was and is seen by many young people as irrelevant, sexist and homophobic. Until quite recently, this has been all too true - not allowing women priests was one obvious example. But in this instance, vast progress has been made in recent years. To-day in the Church of

England, there are some wonderful women priests doing an excellent job, and they now account for over 50% of ordinands. Just recently, to great rejoicing amongst Anglicans, the church has appointed the first female bishops. The Roman Catholic and Russian Orthodox churches have a different tradition on this, based on how they interpret Bible teaching. While the sexist issue has greatly improved in this country, it has to be admitted that in some countries in the Middle East, women are still very much treated as second class citizens. Even here in the Middle East the situation had been starting to improve up until a few years ago. But now with the rise of fanatical fundamentalist groups, the rights of women in some areas have, regrettably, gone backwards.

But it is the Gay Issue that continues to cause major problems. Up until 1967, homosexuality was a crime in the UK and seen as a sin, and then that was the year when it was decriminalized. To-day, happily, society is much more tolerant and enlightened. But there are still major problems in some of the homophobic African Churches and cultures, and in some of the more fundamentalist groups. There are some congregations that have torn themselves apart over this issue, and this is tragic. But to my mind, it is wrong to deny homosexuals, male and female, the comforts of love and companionship. I cannot imagine anything more chilling for a gay person to be told that God loves them dearly but they must live a celibate and lonely life. The same cannot of course be said of paedophilia, to which some parts of the church tragically have turned a blind eye in the past.

Let us look at what the Bible has to say on the topic of homosexuality; this is the sort of verse we find in the book of Leviticus in the Old Testament:

Do not lie with a man as one lies with a woman; that is detestable. (Lev. 18: 22),

and again:

If a man lies with a man as one lies with a woman, both of them have done what is detestable. They must be put to death; their blood will be on both their heads. (Lev. 20:13).

It is this last verse in particular that has caused so much trouble especially for male homosexuals throughout the world and not only just amongst Christian communities. Leviticus is the third book in the Bible, and was about laws or rules for worship mainly for the children of Israel, several centuries BCE. Leviticus 20: 13 is quite outrageous and clearly a non-starter. This is the sort of Old Testament sentence that makes the sceptic even more entrenched in his or her position. This is also a prime example of what I said in Chapter 2, about the fact that we must not take everything in the Bible, especially the Old Testament, to be literally true. Let us now turn to the New Testament, where we find that Paul has quite a lot to say on the subject. Frequently, he has a jolly good rage against any form of sexual immorality, debauchery, drunkenness, orgies and so on:

Do you not know that the wicked will not inherit the kingdom of God? Do not be deceived: Neither the sexually immoral, nor idolaters, nor adulterers nor male prostitutes nor homosexual offenders nor thieves nor the greedy nor drunkards nor slanderers nor swindlers will inherit the kingdom of God. (I Cor. 6: 9 – 10).

This passage is authentic Paul in what was probably one of the first of his letters in the New Testament. In Paul's first Epistle to Timothy, the following verses appear in the first chapter:

We know that the law is good if one uses it properly. We also know that the law is made not for the righteous but for the lawbreakers and rebels, the ungodly and sinful, the unholy and irreligious; for those who kill their fathers and mothers, for murderers, for adulterers and perverts, for slave traders and liars and perjurers – and for whatever else is contrary to the sound doctrine that conforms to the glorious Gospel of the blessed God, which he entrusted to me. (I Timothy 1: 8 – 11).

Some translations substitute *"practising homosexuals"* for *"perverts"* here. There is considerable doubt amongst scholars to-day that Paul was the author of this Epistle. Paul himself has received a poor reputation in some Christian circles. Most of this is undeserved, because it turns out that most of his anti-sex and anti-gay passages come in the later letters that he probably did not write. If the author was someone different and the Epistle was written sometime later, as seems likely to be the case, then this negative feeling shows what was prevalent in the young Church of the time. Indeed the early Church did not approve of homosexuals. There are similar strong sentiments in the first chapter of Paul's Epistle to the Romans, where in verses 18 – 30, Paul raged against all forms of "wickedness, evil, greed and depravity" (verse 29). What are we to make of this? Clearly Paul was against any form of immorality, debauchery and dishonesty and we can happily go along with that. But it does seem that homosexuality was also a no-no if not for Paul, then for the early church.

What about the Gospels and what does Jesus say on this subject? There is nothing in any of the Gospels on the subject of two men or two women together. Jesus has nothing to say at all on the subject. The line is always to love one another. Some scholars have suggested that the story of the healing of the Centurion's Servant as given in the first 10 verses of Luke Chapter 7, may have been a case of a homosexual relationship.

When Jesus had finished saying all this in the hearing of the people, he entered Capernaum.   There a centurion's servant, whom his master valued highly, was sick and about to die. (Luke 7: 1 – 2).

Some translations give *"whom his master valued highly"* as *"who was dear unto him"*.

We cannot tell whether this was a homosexual relationship, but it would have been quite normal in those days for a master and his servant. Anyway, whatever the case, the centurion showed great faith and Jesus had no hesitation in healing the servant, whatever the sexual orientation of the Centurion.

In my view, we should read what Paul has to say, but realise that *Paul was entitled to his own opinions*: he was merely reflecting the strong feelings present amongst his people in the first century A.D. This was what he thought on the subject in his day. We do not have to agree with him.   Furthermore, the position appears to have become even more negative amongst the early church after Paul's time.

There is more and more evidence that homosexuality is a fact of life for certain people of both sexes. Although it has yet to be discovered, I believe it very likely that there is a gene that some people have that makes them homosexual. There is evidence for this in certain families, where there are a greater number of lesbian, gay and bisexual individuals than might reasonably be expected. I believe that it is wrong to try to "correct" their orientation, because this often leads to unhappiness and illness.

The subject of sexuality has caused more stress in the Christian Church in the early part of the 21st century than any other topic. Homosexuality is closely linked in with the idea of same sex marriages. At one end there is the liberal wing who are all in favour of this while at the other end there are a number of African Churches who are dead against the whole idea. There is then the very well-meaning Archbishop of Canterbury, Justin Welby, trying to keep the peace between the two wings. The first stage for Christians is that both sides need to understand that there are those who take a profoundly different view from their own. They need to show respect and love still for those Christians who nevertheless hold a profoundly different view. Then and only then can the Church start to move forward and find the answer. Christianity is not alone on this one: in strict Moslem and Jewish societies, homosexuality is strictly forbidden.

My own view is that there are indeed a number of men and women who are born with the homosexual gene. They should surely be allowed to live their own lives peaceably and form loving relationships with each other. Happily, as I have said, this is much less of an issue than it used to be to the extent that for many people it is now a non-issue. Nevertheless, this issue still exists and cannot be swept under a carpet.

3. Abortion.

This is another tough one. Is it ever right to abort a foetus and if so under what circumstances? Many people might think the issue straight forward: on the one hand there are those who think little of it and they take the view that it is wrong to bring an unwanted child into this world. Therefore, it is best to abort and have done with. They will further argue that if abortion is disallowed, it would simply move underground. Unofficial backstreet abortionists involve a greater danger of injury and damage to women. Furthermore, many will argue that the woman has rights over her own body. At the opposite end of the scale, there are those who take the view that it is simply wrong to abort a living being whatever the reason. This view especially applies to the Roman Catholic and the Eastern Orthodox Faith.

These two extreme views cannot both be right so is there a compromise position? It is possible to argue that the issue will turn on at what stage does the soul enter the foetus. It's a fair question, and if we are honest, no-one knows the answer. It is also a question that is seldom discussed but is surely highly relevant. If it is the case that the soul enters the foetus at the point of conception or at least very soon afterwards, then that soul is denied its chance of a life and abortion would be tantamount to murder. This is the Roman Catholic and Eastern Orthodox position. If on the other hand, the soul enters the foetus at the moment of birth, then we can be more sympathetic towards abortion. My own view here is one that is difficult to justify: I believe that the soul enters the tiny body at some stage between these two extremes – perhaps about three to four months after conception. Much as I would like to, I cannot offer the reader any particular evidence for this belief, but it does, to me, seem not unreasonable. Interestingly, this idea ties in very much with the Muslim teaching, which is that the foetus receives its soul, which is called "ensoulment", 120 days after conception. This means that Islam would only accept abortion after 120 days if the mother's life is in danger. They are not that keen on abortion before 120 days either, but some Muslims would permit it if the child might be born with a serious defect. In addition it does seem likely that in the later stages of the pregnancy, the foetus becomes sentient and that means that it will feel pain.

Given this belief, I cannot support the idea of abortion after about three months, except when continuing the pregnancy is going to severely endanger the life of the mother and thus the foetus. In that case, then a late abortion might be contemplated. If an abortion takes place early in the pregnancy, after only two or three months, or at least as soon as pregnancy is confirmed, then an abortion might be acceptable. I can understand the desire for an abortion after rape or if the foetus is shown to be severely abnormal. Even so it is still not something that I would feel comfortable about.

The way forward is education and worldwide contraception, and then in an ideal world, the issue would not arise. At present, this does not appear to be an issue that is much talked about apart from in the USA with pro-life groups, and in the Republic of Ireland where they have recently legalised abortion for the first 12 weeks of a pregnancy. I predict that in about 50 or so years' time, with greater enlightenment and near universal contraceptive measures being taken, this will cease to be an issue, and abortion will become a thing of the past.

4. Euthanasia.

This is another vexed question that is becoming ever more controversial. Euthanasia is a Greek word that literally means "a good death". With the advance of medical science it is proving ever more possible to keep a human alive but sometimes under intolerable and painful conditions. Thus an increasing number of people are expressing the wish to depart this life quietly and with dignity at the time of their own choosing. Presently, this can be arranged in Switzerland and under certain circumstances in Holland. A few other countries and certain states of America are currently seriously considering the issue. The result is that some people from the U.K. have been taking themselves quietly off to Switzerland and ending their lives with the help of an organisation called "Dignitas".

So, what is the current position in the U.K? At present euthanasia is simply illegal. At this stage it is necessary to draw a distinction between active euthanasia and passive euthanasia. Active euthanasia means the administration of a deadly drug that ends life almost immediately. Passive euthanasia means the administration of a drug specifically to ease the pain and suffering that, as a side effect, might go some way towards shortening the life. Passive euthanasia at least to some degree has now become common place and is something that the great majority can be comfortable with. In 1958, Pope Pius XII declared that for any terminally ill and suffering patient, the doctor may administer a drug to alleviate suffering even if it leads to an earlier death. So this is not really the issue.

If we examine active euthanasia, there are the usual arguments on both sides. On the positive side, active euthanasia provides relief from pain and suffering, which becomes so intense that the patient sometimes feels that he or she would be better off dead. Secondly, the patient has autonomy and actively wills their own death. Some people might add in the economic cost of keeping someone needlessly alive, perhaps costing thousands of pounds each week. On the negative side, there is the intrinsic wrongness of killing. And then there is the so-called "Slippery Slope" argument: once this becomes common place, pressure can subtly be applied by relatives to an individual to "do the decent thing" because of the nuisance value involved and also for financial reasons.

So where does this leave us on active euthanasia? Passive euthanasia does provide us with a suitable grey area that can help in many cases. For myself, I cannot go along with active euthanasia however difficult the circumstances. Palliative care in this day and age does provide considerable relief even if it means heavily sedating the patient. Nevertheless, I think it quite likely that active euthanasia will become more and more accepted in many countries including the U.K. in the not too distant future. Just because something like this becomes generally accepted, this does not necessarily mean that it is morally correct.

Chapter 11:
Three More Important Matters.

1. The Importance of Healing

There are many stories in the gospels of Jesus healing the sick. And it wasn't just Jesus who was able to heal. In the Old Testament, Elijah and Elisha are credited with healing powers. In the Acts of the Apostles, Chapter 3 verse 8, Peter heals a crippled beggar, and there are other stories in Acts of Peter and Paul performing healing miracles. But it is not always that simple. Even Jesus was not always able to heal someone instantly. Two interesting cases I have already described in Chapter 6. The Healing of the Boy with an Evil Spirit, and the Healing of the Blind Man were in two stages.

There are some people who have what we might describe as the Gift of Healing - and it is a gift. These people, often quite humble and unassuming, have a wonderful gift whereby they are able to go a long way towards affecting a healing. But this is seldom instant, unlike most of the stories in the Bible when healing takes place in what seems like a flash. It involves the Laying on of Hands in a peaceful environment often with the aid of prayer, and will usually be a gradual process. Also, healing does not always mean a complete cure for the physical body. It is possible for a person to be healed, and become at peace with him or herself although the physical symptoms of the illness remain. Healing should be seen as complementary to modern medicine and not a last resort if medicine has failed. It is true that some cynics could have a field day on healing with talk about psycho-somatic conditions, but I have met and known a fair number of genuine healers, really good people, who, in their often quiet and unassuming way, do a huge amount of good.

How does all this come about? It is my belief that the healer acts as a channel The power comes from the spirit world and acts through the healer, whether he or she realises it. Harry Edwards (1893 – 1976) was a powerful healer who, in his time, helped many people. He wrote this:

I believe it is true that the philosophers, guides, doctors and inspirers from Spirit, are God's ministers helping to guide human destiny to live rightly in His sight, and, as healing is an effective means of demonstrating spiritual awareness through the healing of sickness, its ultimate purpose is the spiritualisation of mankind.

This implies that there are any number of spirits in the next world, who may or may not have had an existence on Earth, and who are only too anxious to help alleviate suffering and sickness in this world. The way they do it is to act through a channel in this world. Any number of people can act as a healer, but it will only work provided that the healer humbly accepts that he or she is the channel. It is not likely to work if the healer thinks of themselves as a "good" healer or has too much pride in their work. It is also seems possible to me that the power could come through the healer directly from God. I also believe that there are some healers who are not specifically Christian, but nevertheless, God is quite capable of working through these healers, and frequently does so.

I firmly believe that some people have the ability to act as healers. They are wonderful people.

2. The Importance of Music.

"Music is a moral law. It gives soul to the universe, wings to the mind, flight to the imagination, and charm and gaiety to life and to everything." (Plato).

"Knowledge is the food of the soul." (Plato).

"If music be the food of love, play on." (Shakespeare: *Twelfth Night*).

"Music is food for the soul".

The third quotation comes from the opening lines of Shakespeare's *Twelfth Night*, spoken by Duke Orsino of Illyria. The last quotation is of unknown origin, but may be a misquotation or combination of the first three. Anyway, there is a wealth of wisdom here. For so many people, exposure to the right form of music can be a tremendous boost for the soul. It can induce a real "high", or it can relax the body and bring about a lovely feeling of peace. But it has to be emphasised that it must be the right form of music. What may be food for one soul may feel like an obnoxious poison to another! In my own case, there are some truly great pieces of classical and semi-classical music that have this effect, whereas some forms of modern "pop" music are to me just a disturbance, and I want to turn the noise off at once, because it causes great anguish to my soul! Someone else may feel the exact opposite. In addition, the musical instrument makes a huge difference. My favourite instrument is the piano, but for someone else it might be the violin or the electric guitar.

There are plenty of references to music and dancing in the Bible. A good example in the Old Testament comes in Psalm 150. The six verses in this Psalm are full of praise to God and they mention a number of musical instruments:

Praise him with the sounding of the trumpet, praise him with the harp and lyre, praise him the tambourine and dancing, praise with the strings and flute, praise him with the clash of cymbals, praise him with resounding cymbals. (Psalm 150: 3 – 5).

This sounds like a jolly good party! In the New Testament, the singing of a hymn is much encouraged: a good example comes from the time when Jesus and his disciples had finished the Last Supper just before they went out on to the Mount of Olives:

"When they had sung a hymn, they went out to the Mount of Olives." (Mark 14: 26).

The same verse appears in Matthew Chapter 26, verse 30. A second example is the parable of the Prodigal Son, with music and dancing laid on for the young man when he returned home, as told in Luke Chapter 15:

But the father said to his servants, "Quick! Bring the best robe and put it on him. Put a ring on his finger and sandals on his feet. Bring the fatted calf and kill it. Let's have a feast and celebrate; he was lost and is found." So they began to celebrate. Meanwhile the older son was in the field. When he came near the house, he heard music and dancing. (Luke 15: 22 – 25)

St Paul, likewise, is also happy with singing:

"Speak to one another with psalms, hymns and spiritual songs. Sing and make music in your heart to the Lord, always giving thanks to God the Father for everything, in the name of our Lord Jesus Christ." (Ephesians 5: 19 – 20).

Thus, in many church services there is an abundance of hymns and sometimes a psalm, all of which can be wonderfully uplifting, be it at home, school or in the church. Also, funerals now provide opportunities for playing music beloved or meaningful to the recently departed. This can be of great benefit to those who are left behind to mourn the departed. In short, music is a wonderful example of man-made beauty which can be used to bring people together in church or elsewhere.

There was an essential role played by music in the whole history of the liturgy, which began with simple forms of plainsong, and then developed into the wonderful polyphonic compositions of the 16th and 17th centuries. This in turn gave rise to major works such as the settings of the Mass by J. S. Bach, Mozart and Beethoven, which are often nowadays treated as concert pieces, although it is still possible to have a celebration of a Mass with settings by such composers. In this respect, our European culture for classical music has its foundation in the forms and expression of Christianity.

In my view, all young children should be introduced to music at an early age, but as far as possible taking due account of the sort of music that is right for that particular child. I would not support the idea that learning a musical instrument should be compulsory for children, but rather every possible support and encouragement should be given to any child who shows interest. Thus, as many as possible should be encouraged to learn an easy tune on a simple whistle or flute, perhaps leading on to a piano. An electric guitar is also popular as it is relatively easy to learn to play. In addition all children should be encouraged to sing. Some form of dancing is also often popular and should receive the same encouragement. Dancing can be linked to community activity, for example: Maypole dancing, Scottish Country dancing and English Country dancing. And in a more general sense, I would include art and drama here. These can be a hugely important part of some people's lives.

In all my many years of teaching, most classes have contained children who were learning the piano or another musical instrument, and it always seemed to me that such children were calmer and in many ways much more advanced as individuals.

I cannot recall any child involved in music as being troublesome.

3. The Importance of Animals

We live in this world with a mass of animals, some large, some very small, some vicious, some cuddly and some great companions. The first thing to realise is that some animal species are far more highly evolved and advanced than others. Insects have their very necessary purpose as being part of the food chain, but at the other end of the scale, there are dolphins who seem to be very highly evolved and, I would argue, not far short of humans in intelligence, albeit a very different form of intelligence, living as they do in groups with the ability to communicate with each other. Great apes and elephants also appear to be highly evolved, able to recognise each other and communicate with each other. Many of our birds are well able to communicate with each other with their singing and chirping. All are worthy of respect, so what I find particularly painful is the mistreatment of animals by humans. That does not mean that we should all be vegetarian. There are some animals which are here to provide food for us and other animals, but humans must make sure that these animals are slaughtered in a humane way. This by itself is a topic that gives rise to heated debate and passing of laws, for example, Halal meat and Kosher food.

Many animals are referred to in the Bible. I will mention just one example here and that is the sheep, an animal that played a very important part of the possessions of the ancient Hebrews and many Eastern nations generally. The well-known parable of the Lost Sheep states:

"Suppose one of you has a hundred sheep and loses one of them. Does he not leave the ninety-nine in the open country and go after the lost sheep until he finds it? And when he finds it, he joyfully puts it on his shoulders and goes home. Then he calls his friends and neighbours together and says 'Rejoice with me; I have found my lost sheep.' I tell you that in the same way there will be more rejoicing in heaven over one sinner who repents than over ninety-nine righteous persons who do not need to repent." (Luke 15: 4 – 7).

Other animals that are mentioned in the Bible include: bears, leopards, foxes, donkeys, camels, horses, lions, deer, wolves, cattle and snakes. Birds of the Bible include: eagles, vultures, owls, ravens, doves, pigeons, partridges, quails and sparrows.

The question can very reasonably be asked: do animals have souls and if so, would they have an existence after this one? No one knows the answer, and there is nothing in the Bible on this subject, but it does seem to me that in some of the higher species, why ever not?

A special bond can often be formed between a human being and, for example, a dog. This particularly applies when that individual is living a rather solitary existence. Not everyone is enamoured of a domestic cat, and yet, a cat can also become a most wonderful comfort animal. As already stated in Chapter 3, I believe that once we move into the next world, we are met by a relative or close friend who particularly loves us. It may be that a lonely person who did not form any close personal relationships might be met by a loving pet dog which had already "passed over". If some animals have souls, this would seem to be entirely reasonable.

There have been a number of wonderful stories of some evolved animals, such as dolphins, who swim with humans and on occasion save the human from danger. More recently, there was a report in the press of a 4 year old boy playing in front of his parent's house when he was set upon by the neighbour's vicious dog. By pure chance, this scene was captured on video by a security camera. There was then a great flurry of grey fur, and the family cat was seen charging head first into the dog, which, totally taken by surprise, was sent flying. The cat then chased the dog around the corner before returning to see how the small boy was. He was slightly injured, but nothing like as badly as if the cat had not intervened regardless of its own safety. The scene was shown on television news and the story went viral on the Internet and social media. This is just one of many well authenticated stories of animals coming to the rescue. It proves nothing, but surely there are some animals which are here to help us, and are far more advanced than we are apt to give them credit for.

In November 2004, my wife and I enjoyed a lovely holiday in Sri Lanka. The country is beautiful, the people very friendly and they appear to have a wonderful working relationship with a large number of animals on the island. Three weeks after our return, we were shattered to learn of the great tsunami that devastated the coastal areas especially on the east side of Sri Lanka. This was caused by a massive earthquake of magnitude

9 on the Richter scale under the sea off the coast of Sumatra. I referred to this in Chapter 10. The amazing thing is that so many domestic and wild animals seemed to sense what was about to happen and fled to higher ground. Sadly there was a huge death toll amongst humans, but very much less so amongst the animal kingdom. There were numerous stories of animals, in particular elephants, becoming very agitated prior to the tsunami. Somehow, many of these animals just "knew" that something was very amiss.

Animals may be used therapeutically, so there are the "Hospital Dogs" or the "Pat a Dog" schemes where people who have been non-communicating or depressed maybe for psychological or emotional reasons, are visited by a dog and its owner. They have started to talk again often using the animal as the undemanding communication partner. Animals have also been shown to help combat pain. Research at the Loyola University in the United States has shown that having a pet can help patients who have had hip or knee replacements operations, with those that have a pet, on average, needing 50% less painkillers. Also at the University of Minnesota's Stoke Institute cat owners were shown to have a 30% lower risk of death from heart attack than non-cat owners. All the available evidence points to the fact that having a pet is often beneficial in terms of cardiovascular fitness and relieving stress. On top of that, so many domestic animals often give us unconditional love and affection. There is much that we can learn from this.

Finally, before we leave this topic, there is a moral issue that needs to be aired. Should animals be used in medical experiments? This is a tough one and as usual, there is no easy answer. It is undoubtedly true that humans can benefit from experiments done on animals, but it is also true that these experiments can and do cause pain and suffering to the animals. One extreme position will hold that no experiments of any sort should be carried out, but this would greatly hamper the cause of medical research. At the other extreme the view would be that animals are of no value and thus we can do what we like with them. The answer surely lies in some sort of half-way house, that with due consideration the benefits outweigh any pain inflicted on the animal, but nevertheless, any suffering on the animal should be kept to a minimum.

Animals are not perfect but they can teach us so much if only we are prepared to listen to them and treat them fairly. In my experience, so many animals are much more content with where they are in life than so many discontented human beings.

Chapter 12: Conclusion.

In the preceding chapters, I have looked at many of the issues facing Christianity to-day, and tried to indicate possible ways forward. There are many who will conclude that I have only scratched the surface and that there is much more to it. That is a fair point, but I have deliberately tried to keep matters as simple as possible.

Life in this world consists of a series of *challenges* for most people. These challenges come at times when often we least expect them or even least want them. It is not so much what happens to us but rather *how we behave and react to unplanned events*. This is what really matters. It is also true that there are some people who seem to have far bigger challenges than others. It may be that this is what they have chosen for themselves even if they may not realize it at the time. Progress is made when we face up to these challenges and find a way forward. But the way forward is neither linear nor predictable. An analogy of this comes from I call the five door scene, although the number of doors is arbitrary. You come through a door into a room, where you can relax before deciding on what to do next. Ahead there are five doors which are firmly closed. Progress will come on managing to go through one of the doors, when you are ready.

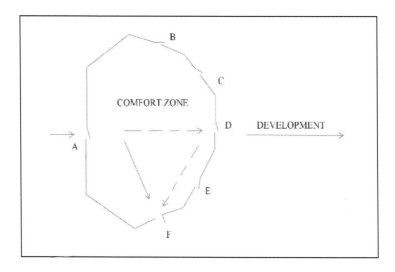

In the rough diagram given above, you have just come through the door marked "A", which is a previous challenge. You have to close the door behind you before it is possible to move on. Progress appears to be in the direction of left to right on the diagram. Thus after a suitable period of reflection, and if you wish, relaxation, in what might be described as a *Comfort Zone*, you look around and see that there are five doors ahead of you all of which are closed. You decide that the natural way forward is through door D which is straight ahead. You then try to open Door D, but it is firmly locked. You pause and then try again but with the same result. You may even try throwing your full weight behind the door, as many do, to force it open but the result remains that the door is firmly locked and bolted. While you are then bewildered and even frustrated by what is happening, suddenly, without warning, you notice that door F has opened and someone (possibly Jesus or your Guardian Angel?) is quietly beckoning you in that direction. This is not

what you were expecting, nor had even planned, and you do not
have to go that way. However, it may be the way you should
go to make progress, and then the process is repeated. It is also
true that door F may not remain open for long. *Those who get
on in life find that they do best to take the opportunities that are
offered when they appear.* Life may appear secure and peaceful
in the Comfort Zone, and some people seem to be content to sit
around there for much of a lifetime, but it is my belief that *life
only begins once you can find a way forward outside your
Comfort Zone.* Progress in this life also equates to the spiritual
development that I mentioned in the section under the Problem
of Evil in Chapter 10, and that spiritual development can only
really get going once one moves outside the Comfort Zone. It
is also worth adding that we sometimes hear people saying that
a disaster or severe life-changing accident was the best thing
that ever happened to them forcing them to re-evaluate their
life. Such is life!

This final section concerns my own personal belief for which
there is little or nothing in the Bible or indeed in Christian
teaching. *It is my belief that each one of us has come into this
world with a **specific purpose**.* In other words, God has a job
for each one of us and it is up to us to find out what that job is.
There is a hint of this in the book of the prophet Jeremiah,
where God says to Jeremiah:

*"For I know the plans I have for you," declares the Lord,
"plans to prosper you and not to harm you, plans to give you
hope and a future."* (Jeremiah 29: 11).

Some will be certain of that purpose or job from an early age.
An obvious example would be anyone who says from an early

age that they know they should be a doctor, surgeon, healer or nurse for example. Other cases might be someone who wishes to be a teacher, craftsman, farmer, or a loving parent, and there are many other very worthy examples that could be stated. Not everyone achieves in this life what had been originally intended and some callings come rather later in life – for example a city banker who later on decides to become a teacher or a priest. It does not have to be a "public" calling, for it could be being the carer of a multiply handicapped child. In my opinion, this last example is a particularly noble calling which can last a lifetime. It is also my belief that some people come into this life to learn a particular lesson, such as tolerance, or learning how to stand on one's own two feet. All this implies some form of existence before this life and why not? This is my answer to the question posed in Chapter 3 about whether or not we have an existence before our lives. It also implies an existence after this life when presumably one's life comes under some form of review. In the end what matters is whether one has made a *difference* and whether one has made the world a better place in however humble a way, or even possibly making the life of one other person in the world more comfortable and bearable. In addition, *we should all do our best to help other people, to care for the earth and to keep it for the people who come after us.* Increasingly, I find my judgement of people depends upon *how they behave, what they achieve and how they treat other people.* In the parable of the Good Samaritan, Luke Chapter 10, Jesus is interested in the actions of Good Samaritan. By comparison, what people profess that they believe in is not that important! I have known some people who have been regular churchgoers and yet, despite what they profess, their behaviour at times is far from being Christian.

"All men and women are equal". Well yes, as far as their existence on earth is concerned. But each person has two parts, their earthly body and their spirit or soul. At death, the body is discarded and it is the soul that moves on. At the soul level, it is my belief that the people are most unequal. In Chapter 4, I talked about meeting the occasional *advanced human*. From time to time, I feel privileged to be in the presence of someone who appears at least to me to be an *advanced human* or *advanced soul*. Perhaps one in about a hundred, these are wonderful and amazing people who immediately make you feel good. They are not usually people with any great wealth, in fact often rather the reverse, and they do not have to be saints. In an often quiet way, they are here to act as a wonderful example. Sometimes their lives last only a few years and they show how as a child they can endure, for example, terminal cancer. In the 1960s and 1970s my family were good friends with an elderly widow whom we can call Violet. She was a calm and peaceful presence who, with her late husband, had been in a prisoner of war camp run by the Japanese. Despite terrible hardships, her spirit never failed and when, so I was told, the spirits of even some of the nuns also captured began to fail, Violet remained indomitable. An example in a more public sphere is Dame Cicely Saunders who died in 2005. This indomitable lady had a difficult childhood during which she realised the plight of the underdog. Against massive odds, she went on to found St Christopher's Hospice and to be the founder of the Modern Hospice Movement. Her magnificent work transformed the management of care for the dying and she introduced the idea of palliative medicine. Another example in the public eye recently is the Pakistani teenage girl Malala Yousafzai who survived a Taliban murder attempt and has quite rightly won the Nobel peace prize for her brilliant campaign to give all children, especially girls, an education. She is a girl in a million.

At the other end of the scale, there are a few individuals whom I would describe as not necessarily evil but who may have done dastardly evil deeds. I do not believe that people are born evil but they may have been born what I call "primitive". Unless they are given very careful help and love, these people can often become evil. What we have to try to do is to see what sort of ways we can find to help them – often not at all easy.

In recent years, we have become increasingly obsessed by a person's Intelligence Quotient (IQ). This is important and makes a huge difference to how someone can progress in life, however, in my view there are two other quotients which are more important. They are Emotional Quotient (EQ) and Spiritual Quotient (SQ). However high one's IQ, that person is not going far if he or she is emotionally immature or selfish, having a low EQ. The SQ is in some ways connected to this. People with a high SQ have a great spiritual presence and awareness. They have a great sense of what truly matters in life and their place in it. This is not confined just to Christians. It is possible to have a high SQ and be a Jew, Muslim, Hindu, Buddhist or other religion or even agnostic or atheist. There are people who think themselves to be highly "religious" and attend church regularly, but who in fact have quite a low SQ. These are the people who claim to be believers but who are arrogant and judgemental. There are some who indulge in what has been called a "Functional Atheism". They profess a belief in God, and may even have quite a high church position, but much of the time they are pursuing worldly goods and have little time let alone love for other humans. At the time of Jesus, these people were the Pharisees and Jesus was often having a go at them.

"Woe to you, teachers of the law and Pharisees, you hypocrites! You are like white washed tombs, which look beautiful on the outside but on the inside are full of dead men's bones and everything unclean." (Matthew 23: 27).

By contrast, people with a high SQ have a wonderful sense of curiosity, humility, empathy, self-awareness, joy and the sheer love of humanity. Again I quote from St Matthew's Gospel:

"Not everyone who says to me, 'Lord, Lord,' will enter the kingdom of heaven, but only he who does the will of my Father who is in heaven." (Matthew 7: 21).

****

Some Christians might take issue with parts of the above paragraphs. I am not able to provide any proofs, but what I will say is that given the above, so many things fall into place. In the end, it is certainly true that a strong faith goes a very long way. If this book has provided the agnostic or atheist with some stimulating thoughts, a desire to seek further, discuss matters with others including those with different faiths and simply ask the question "why?", then at least some of the aims mentioned in the first chapter will have been achieved, and the book will have succeeded.

Finally, I would like to return again to the subject of Love. We have already discussed this in Chapter 4. St Paul at his best wrote about this in his first letter to the Corinthians, where "Love" can be taken to mean "Charity and respect for others":

*And now these three remain: faith, hope and love. But the greatest of these is **LOVE**.* (I Cor: 13: 13).

Likewise we can listen to what Jesus has to say on this subject in St Luke's Gospel:

"But love your enemies, and do good to them, and lend to them without expecting to get anything back. Then your reward will be great and you will be sons of the Most High...." (Luke: 6: 35).

It is my firm belief that we come into this world to **LOVE** and to **LEARN.**

Some people try to do "Good" things in this world in order to achieve fame. That is not the right motivation. Some other people try to do good things on the quiet in order to achieve some "brownie points" in the next world. This is better, but even this may not be quite right. In my view, it was Mother Teresa of Calcutta (1910 – 1997) who had the right idea when she wrote:

*I am not sure exactly what heaven will be like, but I know that when we die and it comes time for God to judge us, he will not ask, "How many good things have you done in your life?" Rather he will ask, "How much **LOVE** did you put into what you did?"*

St Paul and Mother Teresa have surely got this exactly right.

Bibliography of Books Referred to

Richard Dawkins: The Selfish Gene (OUP)

David Filkin: Stephen Hawkin's Universe (Basic Books)

Stephen Hawking: Brief Answers to Big Questions (John Murray)

Stephen Hawking: The Universe in a Nutshell (Bantam Press)

Anita Moorjani: Dying to be me (Hay House)

Gillian Straine: Science and Religion (SPCK)

48343356R10101

Printed in Poland
by Amazon Fulfillment
Poland Sp. z o.o., Wrocław